Soul Vision

*Ensuring Your Life's
Future Impact*

THE INTENTIONAL LIFE TRILOGY

BOOK THREE

Soul Vision

Ensuring Your Life's

Future Impact

Ramesh Richard

MOODY PUBLISHERS

CHICAGO

Unless otherwise marked, all Scripture quotations are taken from the HOLY BIBLE, NEW INTERNATIONAL VERSION®. Copyright © 1973, 1978, 1984 by the International Bible Society. Used by permission of Zondervan Publishing House. All rights reserved. The "NIV" and "New International Version" trademarks are registered in the United States Patent and Trademark Office by International Bible Society. Use of either trademark requires the permission of the International Bible Society.

Scripture quotations marked KJV are taken from the King James Version.

Scripture quotations marked THE MESSAGE are taken from the THE MESSAGE. Copyright © 1993, 1994, 1995, 1996, 2000, 2001, 2002. Used by permission of NavPress Publishing Group.

Scripture quotations marked NASB are taken from the *New American Standard Bible®* Copyright © 1960, 1962, 1963, 1968, 1971, 1972, 1973, 1975, 1977, 1995 by The Lockman Foundation. Used by permission.

Scripture quotations marked NKJV are taken from *The New King James Version.* Copyright ©1979, 1980, 1982 by Thomas Nelson, Inc. Used by permission. All rights reserved.

Scripture quotations marked NLT are taken from the *Holy Bible, New Living Translation,* copyright © 1996. Used by permission of Tyndale House Publishers, Inc, Wheaton, Illinois 60189. All rights reserved.

Produced with the assistance of The Livingstone Corporation (www.LivingstoneCorp.com). Project staff includes Neil Wilson, Ashley Taylor, and Mary Horner Collins, Dan Van Loon

Published in association with Yates & Yates, LLP, Attorneys and Counselors, Orange, California.

Library of Congress Cataloging-in-Publication Data

Richard, Ramesh. 1953–
    Soul vision: ensuring your life's future impact/Ramesh Richard.
    p. cm. — (The intentional life trilogy; bk.3)
Includes bibliographical references.
    ISBN 0-8024-6462-9
1. Christian life. 2. God—Will. 3. Discernment (Christian theology). I. Title. II. Series.
    BV4509.5.R48 2004
    248.4—dc22

                                                                            2004001878

1 3 5 7 9   10 8 6 4 2

Printed in the United States of America

In honor and memory of

LaVerne Wood Gryte

She passionately embraced
God's unique vision for me
and faithfully enabled its implementation
with prayer, counsel and support

Contents

A Word from the Author

A young couple bought a rather old house. Though the house had been through hard times, they were drawn to its colonial lines and saw its promise. It had survived over a hundred years of occupants. Young and energetic, these thirty-year-olds tore into walls, ripped out old linoleum and carpeting, and began to upgrade the fixtures. Regrettably, they noticed that the roof leaked. Now repairing the roof seemed the priority. They were about to make a major investment in replacing the sheathing and shingles when a contractor friend took them aside and told them to take a deep breath.

"I've looked at your place," he said, "and I can tell why you like it so much. Frankly, I don't know if you can restore its glory, but I do know one thing. You've got to change your approach."

"What do you mean?" they responded. "We're doing things as fast as we can, and if we don't fix the roof soon, the work we've done inside will be ruined."

The friend smiled and said, "True enough, but have you looked at your foundation? That's your most serious and immediate problem."

"Yeah, we know the foundation looks bad, but we thought we'd save that repair job for last, . . . since no one can see the mess from the outside."

The contractor shook his head. "In order to renovate and rescue an older house like this, you've got to go back to the same sequence used to construct it in the first place. The builder started with the foundation. If you don't follow this order, and the house has to be lifted later to make repairs, or part of the foundation collapses when you expose it for reinforcement, you will lose much of what you have already put into the house. First make sure the foundation is solid and that the hidden, framing structure of the house is sound before the roof is fixed. Then you can concentrate on the interior upgrades and decorating."

That contractor's wise counsel mimics the process of restoration in my life and in your life. The spiritual life-construction project we are calling the Intentional Life series now enters its third, crucial movement. If you haven't read Books One and Two, *Soul Passion* and *Soul Mission,* I encourage you to read those books first. Though this third book stands alone, it will be easier and better to rebuild your life from the bottom up and inside out than from the top down and outside in.

Flawed Visions

The Taj Group of hotels boasts the finest traditions of Indian hospitality. They back up their boast with performance. Ranked among the best in the travel and tourism industry, you can count on the staffs of these luxurious shelters to show off Indian sights, sounds, smells, services, and splendor. The Web site of the Taj Mahal Hotel, which is on Marine Drive in the city of Mumbai (formerly, Bombay), declares that it is "a gracious landmark facing the Gateway of India. Reputed for its unique architecture, with corridors that resemble art galleries, no two rooms in this [old] wing are alike. The old wing has standard rooms, sea-facing rooms, and superior rooms, all adorned with original artifacts."

Guests arriving at the hotel frequently notice an abnormality. The stately front of the hotel

> *Philosopher to fish, "The purpose of*
>   *life is to reason and become wise."*
> *Fish to philosopher, "The purpose of*
>   *life is to swim and catch flies."*
> *The philosopher muttered,*
>   *"Poor fish."*
> *Back came a whisper,*
>   *"Poor philosopher."*
>
>   ❦ MAX BLACK

does not face the ocean. It's the rear of the hotel that overlooks the sea. To access the front entrance, guests take an unimpressive backstreet.

Credible tradition provides reason for this curiously inverted building. During the British Raj, the architect sent the design of the building from London. The builder took great pains, spent enormous resources, and used the finest materials to erect the imposing and handsome structure. Except, he failed to take the architect's vision into account. After it was built, folklore has it that the architect decided to view his extraordinary design from the deck of the ship that brought him from England. As his vessel made a grand entry into the waters of India's gateway city, he realized what had happened. The hotel had been built, but backward! He saw the unadorned rear of the building facing the ocean. Despondent, he jumped into the waters of the Arabian Sea.

You can access this hotel from the back, but its front faces a common city street, not the magnificent ocean. The builder had followed the flawless design with excellence, but he had not shared the architect's vision. He wasn't "orientated" aright. Yes, as the ads tout, they can arrange rooms inside that provide the guests an ocean view. But the back of building is the front, and the front is the back. The builder was clear about the architect's mission, to build a great building and a lasting tribute, but didn't consider the architect's *vision,* a building that faced the ocean.

In the same way, a random or misorientated life vision is not an appropriate vision for the Christian. Only when our vision and God's Vision parallel each other do we build a beautiful and useful life facing the right direction.

FAULTY VISIONS

Various options present themselves as "valid" future visions. But not all visions for the future are appropriate. Consider the following faulty visions that are built with wrong reference points—well designed but wrongly orientated.

Length of Life

A long life gives you a longer time to accomplish your vision, but life lacks a longevity guarantee. Beyond this reality, even an abundance of years does not guarantee a worthy vision.

"You are ninety-six; your wife is ninety-four. You've been married seventy years. Why think of divorce now?" queried the judge.

The wife piped up, "Actually, your honor, we've been wanting a divorce for fifty years. But we wanted to wait till the children died!"

Living a long life is oriented to the future, as all visions must be, but prolonging life can become an obsession. I know one case where a man contributed to naming a hospital building after himself so he would receive priority of admission and care when he was sick. The Dedman Hospital in Dallas, named after its industrious benefactor, had to be shortened to RHD Memorial because superstition abounded as to how medically helpful a hospital could be with that kind of a name. Indeed, the vision of a chronologically long life without attending morality could justify living simply for its own sake.

Kurt was my age. Had he lived we would still be insulting each other in male jest. Along with his wife and kids (they are the same ages as my wife and kids), I mourned his premature death. He dropped dead while shooting baskets during a lunch break. He seemed to live life to the fullest. A short life but a full life. I also know of those who seek the assistance of suicide doctors because they believe they have lived too long or are petrified of what they may have to endure before death. A long life, with no desire or will to live, cannot be an adequate life vision. Methuselah lived 969 years and not much is said about him. Mere chronological extension cannot validate the vision of life,[1] though a longer life does allow for maturing, at least a maturity forged from mistakes.

Abundance of Possessions

Having lots of stuff—there's a justifiable vision! At least on the outside. A bigger home, better car, finer jewelry. My boys are into cars right now. Later, they'll be into girls. And then they will come to the third stage of the American male—cars again! They know every exotic automotive model in production and can even describe the touted characteristics of futuristic prototypes. Some of their friends drive the cars my boys drool over. I've met the parents of the boys who own the cars my boys covet. They come to me for counsel during marital misery, for life mess ups, for important decisions. Anguish and wretchedness in the richest part of our city is as intense as it is in the poorest neighborhoods. The wealthy experience a different kind of misery, but it is misery indeed.

When the poor are rid of envy and the rich get over greed, they seem to live life better. I have sensed a zest for life in destitute economic situations and a disgust for life in the wealthiest of economies. Net worth doesn't intrinsically enhance life, though a healthy bank balance provides options for repressing circumstantial *physical* misery. Scandinavian countries boast a hundred times the personal income of the Caribbean and a hundred times the suicide rate. A definition of the future shaped merely by the abundance of possessions blurs lofty life vision.[2]

Form of Appearance

I once attended the Cirque Ingenieux. The music hall was filled with people from every walk of life showing off formal splendor. At intermission, I thought I saw circus costumes worn by members of the audience. With the right lighting, music, and movement, my senses could have been dazzled during the break as well. A vision that sets its sights on beautiful appearance doesn't validate life, though the rest of us would rather have you beautiful than not.

Fine clothing allows others to admire you, but an enviable wardrobe doesn't help you view yourself rightly. That's why you've gone after the "personal beauty" vision in the first place. Despite your erroneous premise that clothes make a person, dressmakers make clothes, not the person. Haberdashers make a person look better, but they don't make a person better. They don't make the person at all. Can a vision for beautiful appearance, the need to look good, justify expense of life's energy?[3]

Breadth of Power

Because power carries an aura, some people make the gaining and keeping of power the essence of their future. The hubris that permeates capital cities, from inside the Beltway in Washington to the courtyards of the Parliament House in New Delhi, makes the rest of insignificant humanity sick. Is power the real yardstick of life? Does life really exist inside the intestines of political powerhouses?

The saying goes: "In Bombay, it's where you live; in Delhi, it's whom you know!" Except "whom you know" always changes! In the mid-1990s, India featured three prime ministers in eleven days. Argentina played musical presidents in 2002. No one is permanent, anywhere. Check the growing list of ex-presidents, ex-maharajahs, and ex-prime ministers worldwide. Ex-power brokers are good for ornamental presence as chief guests at social functions, charity balls, and building dedications. If power is perceived by political connections, the links are too weak. Gaining influence and keeping control drives power mongers but is not a worthy vision for life. Your vast connections can make life for others, but they cannot reliably make life for yourself.[4]

Size of Budget

Increasing the budget by a certain percentage each year often becomes a force for living. What a defective gauge of effectiveness! I don't know who really measures life in this way, but one of the first questions leaders ask in measuring the success of other organizations involves the size of the budget. The size of your budget reveals nothing about your income, let alone your stewardship or effectiveness. Revenue is not equal to profitability. The issue is not whether you live within your budget but whether or not you can live within your income. Increasing your income is a better vision than devising a larger budget, but beware of either goal becoming a vision for life.

These revenue increases reveal your ambitions, but putting up large numbers in a budget is not that difficult. What's a billion dollars here or there when you get to be the largest debtor nation in the world? Just because your budget is larger than your neighbor's income doesn't make you better than her—especially if your bank debt is larger than hers. You might as well retreat to "the abundance of possessions" yardstick if you can dole out cash for what you need to have or do. You may not have time to open or play with the toys, but at least you can keep them in storage waiting for life to slow down. Budgets, like fast money, are imaginary, ephemeral figures.[5]

Rate of Growth

Artificial percentage goals are thrown at us as the vision of life's work for next year's performance. To set out a percentage growth goal draws us forward but does not secure performance or results. Every financial prospectus alerts us to "rate of past performance as no guarantee of the future." This philosophy of growth, for example, "doubling next year because we doubled each year over the last five years," will burn you and your company out of life.

Even informed planning does not match prediction. Witness the Asian Tiger economies, whose envious rate of growth burst like a bubble, quaking the world markets at the turn of this century. They boasted incredible rates of economic growth in the late twentieth century. Though they exhibited strong work and money values, they acknowledged lack of character infrastructure (i.e., gross corruption), spelling disaster in the late 1990s. As I write, the global economy is going through market shudders. I've thought of starting a MisFortune 100 list, made up of *former* top-rated companies! Driven by arbitrary growth goals and artificial paper wealth, they live without the direction of character.[6] While goals can motivate and facilitate action toward evaluation of accomplishment, there is no point establishing rates of growth without a valid, ultimate umbrella vision for personal, family, and vocational life. Unfortunately, drivenness itself can become a destination, a vision for life.[7] Rates of growth can be a goal to pursue, but not a vision to live by. Faulty visions face backward and eventually plow into life's brick walls.

Pace of Life

I am finishing up a splendid summer as I write these chapters. Extensive travel on four continents rendered me tired in body but refreshed in soul. I saw thousands of people derive energy from what I shared with them. But I can't take pride in busyness. During my hectic academic year, people ask if I am busy in the summers too, away from professorial responsibilities. Summer changes routines, but the pace remains. I can't measure effectiveness by busyness. Busyness in life is not sufficient evidence of effectiveness in the business of life.

If you do not have the vision for your life already growing, you will tend to equate motion with meaning and mistake activity for purpose. A fast pace in a tough race without direction doesn't bring you the gold medal. You may win at work with busyness but lose life in the process. Measure your pace.[8] Is it a measured pace after the right vision?

Kinds of Recreation

Golf keeps life from becoming a groan. A lake house with boats, four-wheelers, and Jet Skis provides variety in an otherwise monotonous life. Vacation travel on cruise ships feeds body and soul but primarily body. The opportunity to indulge in recreation, whether windsurfing or net surfing, are privileges not given to most of the world. If we equate worthy vision with the kind of recreation a person can pursue and possess, then most of the world is left out of living a worthy life. People I meet in other countries often point to their lacks as reasons for a morbid existence. I grant their complaint. Yacht people have it better than boat people. However, I know some boat people who wake up every morning brimming with intentionality, and I know some yacht people thwarted by purposelessness. When "play" becomes a desperate diversion from frustration rather than the simple enjoyment of a good thing, then life has stopped being meaningful. When recreation becomes a necessity, then it has turned into the very monster from which it was supposed to bring relief—the lack of choices. If our "toys" don't re-create energy for work but instead bring on dread at the prospect of work, then our vision for recreation must be evaluated.

Note that the value of recreation in the structure of life can be good for the basement/foundation. A soul's passion can be energized by the reality and sheer beauty of God's creative handiwork as revealed during a long walk over eighteen holes of golf. Recreation can even provide the means for revitalizing ongoing missions. Yet, for all its temporary enjoyments, recreation cannot be the reason for life. Enjoy your recreation, vacation, and toys because God "richly provides us with everything for our enjoyment,"[9] but don't live for them by justifying your fondness for luxury with that verse. You could wrongly turn them into a vision of life.

Significance of Ministry

I raise this issue of ministry, and two attendant philosophies of life, because Christian leaders often make positive judgments from the apparent numerical and geographical extent of my ministry. The assumption is that "small" ministries in remote places are not successful. Nothing could be further from the truth.

For instance, I know ministers who make vocational decisions based on "how many more people" one can reach in a given situation. The principle of "joining God where we see Him working" or "where He is blessing us" can make our prejudicial interpretation via personal satisfaction or eventual significance the criterion for decisions in ministry focus. I like that principle for a start, but not as a way to determine "stay" or "stick-to-itiveness." That criterion helps identify, test, and confirm one's gifts but does not do much to enable long-term usefulness for God. "Seeing where God is working" serves as a wonderful slogan—except we can't see where God is working most times. Further, we can justify anything we see as "God working," only we can't trust our judgments. Worse, our definition of "God working" is often defined by pragmatic ideas or results—e.g., God doesn't seem to be working where the results are few. Unfortunately, "God's blessing" or "working" often is evaluated by quantity, numbers, and externals—more by circumstances than by calling. Then leaders and their boards go on to say, "God doesn't seem to be working here so it is time to quit," thereby missing out on the key character issues of perseverance and faith.

If a person is looking to *begin* to serve God, he or she should look for where God is working as a *start* but then should go on to consider the less perceivable, less obvious, or less easy options for more effective service—but all in the overflowing use of spiritual gifts under His calling. Neither Abraham nor Paul (nor Moses or Isaiah) used the methods of finding significance or God's direction where they *saw* God working. Most often they did *not* see God working at all. Instead, they "joined God" in the most difficult of circumstances according to His calling, regardless of sight or cost.

Missionary William Carey, at great personal disadvantage, joined God in a place where God didn't seem to be working—at least no one could discern it in the "resistant" fields of India—and his efforts with God continue to bear fruit two hundred years later. Finding significance by joining God in His obvious work is not a philosophy to practice but merely one proof of God's providence, looking *backward*. You can later say, "Now I see that I joined God where He was working!" rather than strive to find God's locale for ministry by that principle of discovery.

Not only does this "significance" yardstick leave out millions of faithful Christian workers in hard and small places; it puts extraordinary pressure on us to somehow make ourselves significant for God. God doesn't want *you* to bring the significant life into being. He wants a faithful and abandoned life that He may cause to become significant in His way.[10] Your way to your significance is not His way, and His way to your significance may not be your way. His ways are higher than your ways and may be contrary to your ways. You may actually settle for less than He intends for your life by attempting to create your significance.

This model of shaping a life vision—moving from early life success to later life significance—also does not account for the suffering a minister may go through. Suffering is seen as an intruder into the successful ministry that one *must* supposedly pursue, when God may actually be making the person's ministry *in* the suffering. How else can we justify the sad saga of persecuted Christians worldwide who, in many cases, are the most "significant" Christians we know? God's first commandment deals with our love for Him, not how significant we can be for Him. Let God decide how significant you are going to be in His economy. You decide how useful you are going to be for Him.

As you know by now, these superficial yardsticks are patently false in validating future vision. Their presence or absence does not really matter in an ultimate, long-range scheme of reality. External scales are relative to person, time, and culture. A person may possess the same degree of satisfaction from one income, one toy, one dress, as another would receive from a hundred of these make-believe indices to success and significance.

FUZZY VISIONS

Faulty visions may be replaced by what I call fuzzy visions. These are more meaningful benchmarks of a life vision. Let's consider these. No one would dispute the deeper quality of life offered by the following items.

Vigor of Health

Health is a far better measuring rod of a solid vision than length of life. Who among us takes good health for granted? I am guilty. Who among us desires a healthy life? I raise my hand along with you. Yet I recall meeting a brilliant and famous Christian composer, twisted in body, gnarled in hands, and confined to a motorized bed for years. With perfect pitch, he would call out the notes, melody, arrangement, accompaniment, and all, as his wife picked them out on the bedside piano. Having sung his songs since my teenage years, I went to his home to encourage him and out came the booming baritone with his signature affirmation, "Nothing is impossible when you put your trust in God."

Good health is wonderful but not necessary for a full life. Vigorous health is preferable to illness. It is a blessing but not necessary for a valid future orientation.[11] If quality of life becomes the vision of life, then the immoral euthanasia movement becomes ethically enticing.

Clarity of Intellect

I hope I never lose it—the most amazing faculty of the human being—the life of one's mind. If I have to choose between a decaying body and a renewable mind, I choose the latter. When a friend was offered the choice of matter over mind, he replied, "Never mind, it doesn't matter!" Clarity of mind and education of the intellect is a magnificent blessing to self and others. Yet devious minds are very clear about their hideous purposes. Darkened minds are unambiguous concerning their pursuits. The terrorists of the world are not dummies.

Instead, your mind must be informed by goodness and wisdom. A sharp mind mixed with a faulty heart always loses out to badness. Knowledge must grow into wisdom. An advanced intellect does not make or portray a renewed mind.[12] Gaining "smarts" without goodness, without a valid future vision, is not faulty, but it is badly blurred. Pursue continuing education, update your profession, develop your credentials, but do not make those the vision of life. They may, however, enable you to accomplish the vision of God for your life.

Quality of Friends

Beginning with my wife, most of my friendships are solid, long term, and mostly unattached. I am able to show and receive attention without difficult and conflicting secondary motives. God has blessed me with thoughtful, generous, and loving friends. The number of them increases each day, but numbers don't matter. Some move from the inside to the outer circles of friendship, while others move in, but all of them are friends all right. I could call on any number of them in a crisis and they would show up. They assure my family of their love when I head off on a long trip, for which I am truly grateful. With most of them, we share more than an accidental, social acquaintance. We see a providential intersection of lives. In some way, small or big, we are enabling each other to fulfill each other's vision for life. Most of them know the larger purposes for which they live. While they make an excellent circle of friends, I cannot sustain quality, insider friendships unless we become resources to each other's life vision.[13] Loners live meaningless lives. Life must be enriched by friendships, but making friendships is not the vision of life.

Neither the philosopher nor the fish in the title quote of this chapter's heading are right. They emphasized and empathized with each other about purposeful monotony in life. Life must be larger than mission. It must carry a focused vision.

Focused Vision

[handwritten: Kathy Harrison — must c clearly — Prv. 21:1-6 — Wisdom w/o power frustrated — power w/o wisdom — misled]

A very angry woman stormed up to the desk of the receptionist for an eye surgeon.

"Someone stole my wig while I was having surgery yesterday," she complained.

The doctor came out and tried to calm her down.

"I assure you that no one on my staff would have done such a thing," he said. "Why do you think it was taken here?"

"After the operation, I noticed the wig I was wearing was cheap looking and ugly."

> *Great minds have purposes; others have wishes.*
>
> ※ WASHINGTON IRVING

"I think," explained the surgeon gently, "that means your cataract operation was a success."

Good vision not only clears up our deficiencies but also helps us realize how our poor eyesight affected others. Once corrected, we not only comprehend how badly we saw but how badly we looked! A focused vision can cure faulty and fuzzy vision. It benefits others greatly.

How may we move from soul mission to soul vision? From flawed to focused vision? Further, how does one validate a life vision? Find the reference point? Select the right orientation?

Before we go into those questions, let's identify, examine, and validate this "vision" word. The ability to validate a future vision—a peculiarly human trait in the pecking order of animal life—allows us to evaluate, value, and assess life. Nonhuman animals do not think about the future, let alone establish a vision around which to orient life.

One's life vision should be validated because humans are given the following tools that beg wise usage. Human beings have:

> ### The faculty to study the present

We are able to examine life, our life. Though we may not be in touch with our motives, we can take an inventory of our gifts, talents, and other resources we possess. We know when we are dissatisfied with life. We can point to stress factors. We know what we enjoy. We can list what we want. We can evaluate options to manage obstacles. We can act to balance life.

> ### The capacity to interpret the past

We are able to look at the past to understand, interpret, and draw conclusions from events and circumstances. We desire to find the meanings and implications of the past for the future. We record, subconsciously or self-consciously, the high and low points of life. We may acquire wisdom from sins we've committed, the mistakes we've made, and the experiences we have had.

> ### The opportunity to pursue the future

Those who have not given up on life—there are some

who exist having died—can still pursue a future vision, intentionally. We possess the penchant to plan, to worry, and to execute. We hope for the best and seek for what tomorrow may bring.

Mere animals may evaluate life by food consumption, playtime, material protection, and limited knowledge—a single dimensional life. Humans are complex and multidimensional. They measure life by a divinely constituted *both/and* in the image and imitation of God. Add awareness of history (before, now, and later) and geography (here and there), and we are able to "number" our days. Therefore, non-Christians can come up with good but fuzzy visions for the future. While we all possess the human faculty of future vision, we must also acquire the distinctly Christian faculty of future vision, which comes from a right relationship with the Lord and His Word.

WISDOM FRAMES VISION

The Bible clearly calls us to measure our days—that includes our past, present, and especially the future—and calibrate life accordingly. Teach us, Lord, to number our days in gaining a heart of wisdom.[1] Check the scriptural points that follow. Wisdom invites us to consider a godly vision for the rest of our life.

Our *frailty*, feebleness, and fragileness, God's Word says, provoke us to number our days. Our days are numbered by God and they are flying by fast.[2] The psalmist prays, "Show me, O LORD, my life's end and the number of my days; let me know how fleeting is my life" (Ps. 39:4).

Wisdom calls us to understand what our end will be. Moses' great commission to the people of Israel includes discernment about our earthly ends as a critical ingredient of strategic wisdom.[3]

The *imminency* of the coming of the Lord Jesus, personally at our death or for the whole earth at His second coming, calls us to wisely watch, wait, and work.[4] Jesus introduced the concept of working during the day while it is light, for night is coming when no one can work (John 9:4).

We live in seductive, *morally evil* days and therefore must make the most of every opportunity in life for God in witnessing for Christ. We must understand the will of the Lord in seizing all circumstances for God.[5]

Measuring our life in all its dimensions and its days is a wise move for us. That's how we can live intentionally today and pursue tomorrow purposefully. The whole Bible urges us to pursue, search, and find wisdom from the Lord. God carries on an instructional ministry in our life through wisdom.

Listen to God's and wisdom's invitation, origin, and promise:

> My son, if you accept my words and store up my commands within you, turning your ear to wisdom and applying your heart to understanding, and if you call out for insight and cry aloud for understanding, and if you look for it as for silver and search for it as for hidden treasure, then you will understand the fear of the LORD and find the knowledge of God. For the LORD gives wisdom, and from his mouth come knowledge and understanding. (Proverbs 2:1–6)

A quality life is more than economic. To an extent, we can measure quality (health) by quantity (thermometers), but gladness of heart with material stuff can keep us from reflecting on life.[6] Quantifiable measurements of life can only detect the lack of quality and cannot measure positive quality. That takes God's wisdom.

An inner sphere must take precedence over the outer sphere, for the inner, spiritual life controls the outer, physical life. Behavior is sourced in the heart.[7] "Above all else, guard your heart, for it is the wellspring of life" (Prov. 4:23). The inner life is the starting point; the outer life is the acting point. Your chemical composition doesn't change the moment after you die—only life is missing! The external action ceases; the internal life continues. Humans, though material, are more than material. Life is both physical *and* spiritual. The two aspects are connected integrally and carry immediate bearing on each other. "A heart at peace gives life to the body, but envy rots the bones" (Prov. 14:30).

Knowledge deals with mental ability and intellectual capability. But wisdom brings the very mind of God to the circumstances and challenges of life. Biblical wisdom provides perspective, strategy, and a worldview because you are rightly related to the God of wisdom. It is *intellectual* for it gives you understanding. It is also *practical* for it helps you live life. God's wisdom is *theoretical* because you use it to find an approach to life, but it is also *applicational* as you bring your Creator's judgment to bear on life's situations. Wisdom will help you understand, experience, and choose God's will. It gives you skills in life. You will possess the skill of knowledge and prudence accompanying the capacity to understand what is best in a given situation. Add to that the faith lessons you will learn from life's experiences.

Biblical words related to "wisdom" give you the ability to understand the dimensions of a decision, discern between competing alternatives, and enable you to arrange them into a pleasing whole. God desires to give you this kind of wisdom in the trials of life:

> If any of you lacks wisdom, he should ask God, who
> gives generously to all without finding fault, and it
> will be given to him. But when he asks, he must
> believe and not doubt, because he who doubts is like
> a wave of the sea, blown and tossed by the wind.
> That man should not think he will receive anything
> from the Lord; he is a double-minded man, unstable
> in all he does. (James 1:5–8)

In order to measure life rightly, we must have a desire to
discover and validate future vision. It takes wisdom—God's
wisdom—to produce a life both full and flourishing. It takes a
right relationship to God in fear and faith, awe and anticipation, which are brought under His purposes. Human (godless
or anti-God) wisdom is foolish (1 Cor. 1–3) because it sub-
scribes to human standards for validating life, human ways of
approaching God, and human paradigms for doing life.
Human wisdom ought to be abandoned. We were redeemed
from an empty way of life (1 Pet. 1:18). Instead, we must "take
hold of the life that is truly life"[8] and grasp the full blessings
of the life that God has already created in and for us.

The crucial resource for a purposeful future life—an
intentional life of reflection, prescription, and application
under the lordship of Christ—is the wisdom and power of
God. If we possessed wisdom without power, we would be
frustrated. If we had power without wisdom, we would be
misled. Christ is both the wisdom and power of God to all
who believe (1 Cor. 1:24). He gives us God's perspective and
power for every issue we face.

You will gain a true yardstick for life from being oriented
to God. Do you seek His consistent input, ongoing perspective,

and effective role for your future life? If you can't measure vision without wisdom, and if you can't have wisdom without God, and if you can't have God without Christ, you better be oriented to Christ in order to approach life in all His/its fullness. Eternal life in present life is to know "the only true God, and Jesus Christ, whom God has sent" (John 17:3). For the complete fulfillment of our being, we must know God. This, said Jesus, constitutes eternal life. "Not only is it endless, since the knowledge of God requires an eternity to develop fully, but qualitatively it must exist in an eternal dimension."[9] This Jesus Christ orientation from a Jesus Christ foundation leads to a purposeful life for the Lord Jesus Christ.

Unfortunately, even followers of Christ can forfeit drawing upon the very resources that must sustain a purposeful life. I don't want that fate to befall any of us. Fortunately, however, and contrary to the dominant metaphor in our trilogy, people are not buildings. The Creator's design has taken our ineffective life-building practices into account. When we fall from the glory of God, our backs face the ocean like the wrongly built hotel. As long as we remain that way, life seems disoriented. Repentance, however, at enormous cost to God and to us, allows us a change of orientation. Once we are rightly oriented, we can move forward into the future.

Moving forward into the future brings us to the final aspect of the Intentional Life—developing our soul's vision. We have talked about our underlying *passion*, loving God, and our ulterior *mission*, glorifying God. The third aspect of intentional living is our *vision*—the ultimate *vision* for the rest of our life.

PLANNING IMPLEMENTS VISION

"Do you have a vision?" I once asked a group of leaders.

One of them confessed, "Have vision? The only vision I have is a television!"

Another remarked, "Thank God for days in which to rest and nights in which to sleep" to match Newton's first law—"An object at rest wants to stay at rest!" One person's vision was leisure; another's was rest. Both were faulty and fuzzy.

The word *vision* simply means "sight" and has to do with the structure and function of the human eye. In common parlance, we talk about the person with poor vision as one who cannot see. Or if a person experiences visions frequently, we may send him off for psychiatric care. In leadership circles, however, the meaning of vision has shifted from "sight" to "foresight." To prevent sophisticated soothsaying about the future, we add the qualities of intelligence and competence to "*vision*ary" leaders. That mental image of the future could become utopian idealism, so we also want discerning and sensible *vision*aries.

Given the dimension of the future that no human can behold, predict, or control, there is only one true visionary—God Himself. We are deceiving ourselves if we think we can prophesy from the past into the future.

Why do the biggest financial investment firms protect themselves with disclaimers about the future as not guaranteed by past performance? Because they can't forecast.

Why do long-range plans get quickly consigned to the shelves of chief executive officers and dusted off for annual review? Because they can't foresee.

Why can't futurists distinguish between fads and trends? Because there are no true futurists. They can't foretell. They can't make the future happen. They may be able to estimate the future with "foretokens," but they cannot anticipate it by foretelling. We've been wrong in making predictions in so many ways before—with bad and good results—that we ought to humble ourselves when we speak about the future. We can build for the future without building the future. We can humbly estimate and extrapolate the future without pridefully generating or guaranteeing it. But, at last report, there is only One true futurist.

Therefore, we acknowledge our status as humans. We can far more easily define our daily mission than articulate a definite future. We know the business (mission) we are charged with—glorifying God in all of life. Coming up with a personal vision for the future, however, is a bit more uncertain and contingent. While pursuing the intentional life, we are very limited. We must get rid of any notions of creating the future.

Yet we also acknowledge our role as humans. We can influence our futures—what we sow we will reap—though we can't determine our tomorrows. Tomorrow must take care of itself.

The Scriptures ask us to face "tomorrow" in two basic ways:

1. Face tomorrow without anxiety because of divine providence.

Anxiety assumes too much responsibility for the future. The tenor of the Lord's words brings assurance to the most fearful person (Matt. 6:25–31). "Do not be anxious, do not fear, do not worry" about tomorrow. A good God sees and supervises the future. He will sustain you in the present, just as He cares for the birds and the flowers, and will sustain you as the future becomes present.

God's providence leads us to God's program for history.[10] Our view of supervised history finds "eschatological" resolution. The first fruits of a glorious future have already been detected and promised in the first advent of the Lord

Jesus Christ. History was bisected by the Incarnation as proof of what is yet to come when the Lord Jesus returns. Consequently, we live in hope of solutions and resolution of the questions and quandaries of personal and macrohistory.

This "already-not-yet" phenomenon corresponds to collecting baggage after an international flight. Last summer, after traveling for thirty-six hours, my family waited two more hours for our baggage to arrive. I was looking for the signs of one of the seven pieces as proof that the others got on board, as promise of the rest to come. To our chagrin, not a single piece arrived. On our return trip, we were elated as the first one showed up. That bag offered proof and promise that the rest of the luggage was loaded onto the plane. The first coming of the Lord Jesus is proof and promise of His second coming. We are in between the time of the early bags and the final bag. We face the future without anxiety. We face tomorrow in hope. Not in soft hope as in, "I wish I could pass my exams even though I didn't prepare." We wait in hard hope, "I confidently anticipate the rest of the story."

God's future vision influences how I live today—my hope, my morality, my perseverance. Much like a bride waits for her wedding day, a student works toward graduation day, and a wife watches for her husband's return, we wait, work, and watch for the final coming of Christ. We face tomorrow with hope, not anxiety. God's providence guarantees His future, the proof of which arrived in Jesus Christ. God's prophecies are not platitudes. They are definite promises. His vision is His mission. He carries out His program to accomplish the purpose of His glory.

What is His program? His vision? Hold on until the next chapter. Meanwhile, God's Word asks us to deal with the immediate future in a second way too.

2. *Face tomorrow with planning, not fatalism.*

We do not predict the future, neither are we resigned to it. We wait, but we also work toward the future. This "planning" is not a straight number forecast that planning departments of large companies undertake. What do they do? They take the last three (or five or ten) years of numbers to graph and project the future. I have to gently alert our organization that because donors gave the last three years doesn't mean they will give this year or that new donors will not emerge. Just because we have historically received a large portion of our income in December doesn't mean it will happen this year. While we can wait until December, we must work for December, allowing God to surprise us with greater or lesser income.

Christian planning sometimes assumes a straight-line cause and effect. Time is linear, but growth is not. We regress or progress even though time marches on. Galatians 6:7 does not say "whatever you sow, you *must* reap." It says that what you sow, you *will* reap, especially in the context of doing evil and good. Yet all this is in the context of a personal God who is not mocked. The sowing/reaping law of harvesting is not governed by an impersonal, fatalistic karmic law but by a personal, just God who will always do right.

Now comes the practical question in terms of the future, especially in developing a personal life vision. We already discussed this matter earlier and do so once more. How much do we really affect the future? Why should we plan if the future is already planned? If that question leads to a spirit of submission to God's plan (James 4:7), God welcomes our humility. A spirit of pride in predictive control, not modified by "if it is the Lord's will" (James 4:15), is arrogant, obnoxious, and opposed by God (James 4:6). God plans without me!

Yet if our practical question arises from a fatalistic resignation, then we leave ourselves out of God's plans, which included our leaving ourselves out. But God's plans include you and me—whether we include ourselves or not. God has much to say about passivity, sluggishness, and laziness—all character traits that often pass for fatalism. Further, the Bible clearly asks us, by precept and pattern, to plan for the future. To not plan when building a house is shameful and wasteful. We must be like the ant who provides for winter by saving in the summer. Proverbs 16:1 puts the balance into planning. We make plans, but it is God who establishes them. You must think about tomorrow, but you mustn't be anxious about tomorrow.

One Friday I happened to be the last faculty appointment for Wilfred, a powerfully focused, thirty-three-year-old Ghanaian student at Dallas Theological Seminary. An accomplished man, the first in his village to go to college, he translated the New Testament into his mother tongue. We discussed his future. Should he pursue doctoral studies or go home to start a ministry? He decided to go home for the next several years and then chase a Ph.D. He wanted me to come to his country once he got there. With a smile that could melt a terrorist, his final words were, "See you at home." Sadly for me, God had a different meaning of Wilfred's word "home." He was hit and killed by a drunk driver that night. Our theological community wept at this loss with "why" questions galore. We have no explanations yet.

Willie constantly reminded us that "God works without me," a saying that grips me often. *God works without me.* His ways are mysterious. He doesn't depend on me for the execution of His plans. Yet He includes and accepts me as a colaborer. These days I add to and share my dead friend's concept in a twin saying: "I work with God, but God works without me." I plan for the future, but God plans without me. I depend on God for my plans to be established, but God doesn't depend on me for His plans to be established.

WORLDVIEW GOVERNS VISION

I close this introduction to soul vision, the final component of the intentional life, with a comment on a Christian worldview for a life purpose. A Christian worldview provides the orientation for life, a reference point by which we live, on which we build, and toward which we move. The Christian way of life corresponds to the Christian view of life. The Christian view of life (as do other views of life) comprises the following components:

➢ *Origins—Where did I come from?*

   I am created by the hand of God, distinct from any other creature in all of reality.

➢ *Identity—Who am I?*

   I am rescued from sin, have been incorporated into a community, and am being prepared for total fulfillment in the future.

➢ *Destiny—Where am I going?*

   Biblical eschatology, whose proof and promise came with Jesus Christ, ends up with a historical teleology that spills into an unimaginable eternity with God. Since my eternal life commenced with Jesus' salvation, it will continue forever in God's presence.

➢ *Morality— How do I live?*

   I live in the present with love for God and concern for people; with faith, building on God's values for my life; with hope, looking forward to a permanent resolution of all questions, quandaries, and conundrums; and with love, practicing Christian virtues in the daily responsibilities of life.

> *Meaning—Why am I here?*

To understand and accomplish God's plans for this world. His plans include me.

The fact that God has plans gives me confidence and hope. The fact that He includes me in His plans provides motivation and responsibility.

Validating a future vision doesn't fall to an economic, numerical, quantifiable model of unintentional and unbridled growth. Solomon experimented with visionary expansionism—in wealth, work, women, and wine—and found it to be whim and wind. Air bubbles floated and fluttered by, for there was no substance to vanity. Instead, constructing a vision for life, like forming one's passion and mission, is a whole life, total life venture that includes a future life undertaking. It carries quantitative and qualitative aspects; connects the outer to the inner sphere; features material and immaterial dimensions; needs knowledge and wisdom. Such life construction integrates personal passion, mission, and vision—the Intentional Life.

VISION COMPLETES PURPOSE

So let's clarify the "vision thing." If vision requires foresight and is based on the future, we ought to gain insight into a future articulated by the Divine Visionary. As we saw in Book Two *(Soul Mission),* the ulterior purpose in all creation is to glorify God. That purpose is the base anchor for the vision. Purpose and vision are related to each other but are not synonymous, as this equation shows:

Purpose = Passion + Mission + Vision

Purpose is comprehensive and ongoing. Vision relates to the future, pulls us forward, and influences our orientation in building the design. In order to construct a personal vision, we must grasp God's Vision for the world and fall in line with it so that the ultimate purpose becomes our personal purpose. Otherwise, like the Bombay hotel building, we'll build a wonderful life the wrong way around.

Soul Vision, Sole Vision

The most distinguished astronomer at the turn of the nineteenth century, Sir Percival Lowell, was particularly known for his expertise on the water canals of Mars. He built his theory on Italian astronomer Schiaparelli's drawings and surmised the canals were constructed by intelligent beings who once inhabited the red planet.

NASA scientists now know Mars much better than Lowell ever hoped to know. They have sent sophisticated probes and rovers to map its dusty and desolate terrain, but haven't found a single canal or water channel yet. Meanwhile ophthalmology has

> We are
> as we come to see
> and as that seeing
> becomes enduring
> in our intentionality.
> ℞ STANLEY HAUERWAS[2]

also advanced in the knowledge of the human eye since 1900. "The canals, as it turns out, are mostly chance alignments of dark patches that the eye, at the limit of resolution, tends to string together in lines."[1] Lowell thought he was studying Mars when all he was doing was mapping the blood vessels in his own eyeballs.

We, too, can suffer from a similar, strange, spiritual eye disease, when it comes to identifying and pursuing God's

Vision for us. We can equate vision with the things nearest to us, demands urgent to us, stresses pressing in on us in personal, family, and work life. We construct grand goals for these three areas and think we are seeing far out there. But without good "eyes" we can't see at all. We need to be occupied with these areas of life for the glory of God. Our daily mission is not to be our life vision. We need surgical relief from the spiritual eye disease that causes the symptoms of equating the near with the far, substituting mission for vision, exchanging the penultimate with the ultimate. Let's conduct a spiritual sight exam as we study God's Vision for the whole world, for all people, for all history and geography.

If the mission of God and the Bible is to bring glory to Himself, the vision of God and the Bible is to bring people to Himself.[3] Bringing people to Himself was not a new thought from the lips of Jesus when He commissioned making disciples worldwide (Matt. 28:19–20). The Great Commission simply reiterates and reinforces God's vision for the world from the beginning. If passion relates to the person of God, and mission to the program of God, then His vision reveals the plan of God for the world. Let me highlight biblical support for God's vision to bring all people to Himself—the central story line of the Bible.[4] God has pursued a whole-earth, all-peoples vision from the beginning and calls us to align with His vision. It is my hope that as you come to see God's purpose for His people and the planet, that the (in) sight will become enduring in your intentionality.

ADAM TO ABRAHAM: AN INTERNATIONAL PAST (GENESIS 1–11)

Before the world was international, it was human. The archetypal period from Adam to Abraham included several themes that have affected the rest of history. Adam, the first man, stood for all the world. As original man, he was representative man. As the first person, he was international in every way—the taproot of the human ancestral tree to which we all ultimately trace our descent. As first sinner, he plunged humankind into a humanly insoluble disaster. He represented all people in his fall and added sin to the genetic makeup he passed on to all people who would ever inhabit the earth. When God asked Adam, "Where are you?" (Gen. 3:9), it was an invitation to Adam's personal repentance but also contained God's offer to the entire world of people who would follow Adam in repentance and return to Him.

In Genesis 3:15 we find the first intimation of ongoing conflict between *all* humanity and the enemy serpent, with the final victory going to the seed of the woman. This verse is sometimes called the *proto-euangelium,* "the first gospel," since the solution to the human race is promised in that embryonic form. When God clothed Adam with the skin of animals (3:21), God's first blood sacrifice anticipated the final blood sacrifice for all people ever to be born in and under the Adamic family—in other words, all of us.

Human alienation from God and from each other continued with advancing, cumulative depravity. Family (Cain and Abel, chap. 4) and social estrangement resulted in proliferation of death (chap. 5), but a godly line emerged to parallel human wickedness. People began calling on the name of the Lord early (4:26) and those like Enoch walked with God (5:22). But the stench of wickedness and evil intent nauseated God, who declared that He would blot out human beings from the face of the earth (6:5–7). A universal flood wiped out all of life, except for Noah, his family, and the animals he brought on board his ark (7:7–9). God's covenant with Noah focused on the entire earth. His three sons began the repopulating process. The tower of Babel narrative (Gen. 11) ends with the confusion of languages and diffusion of peoples across the earth.

Human representation during our "international past" in Genesis 1–11 is not flattering or promising, except for those who call on God, walk with Him, and obey Him. Those who do not call on the Lord, the Creator God, become candidates for permanent judgment. But God's Vision to rescue humanity can be seen and understood from the very beginning of human history.

ABRAHAM TO MOSES: AN INTERNATIONAL COVENANT (GENESIS 12–50)

Babel set the stage for Genesis 12, where God's international vision was covenanted and His international saving theme was repeated. A network of international salvation began with Abraham, continued through the Abrahamic line (e.g., Isaac, Jacob, Judah, David, Jesus), and culminated in the Lord Jesus and His church.

Visit Genesis 12 briefly to view Abraham, the *international* patriarch. God was working with humanity before the Hebrews appeared. Abraham himself was not a Jew, though he began the Jewish race. Verses 1–3 carry two imperatives, each followed by three promises. The Lord said to Abram, "Leave your country." Remember that countries and languages came into existence only after Babel. Abraham belonged to a country, but he was to "go forth from your country, and from your relatives and from your father's house, to the land which I will show you"(12:1 NASB). This land had not been created in the dispersion of Babel (cf. the

Table of Nations in Gen. 10).

God promised Abraham, "I will make you a great nation." A nation that had not yet been created, because this nation was to "be" for other nations. Abrahamic blessing, in spite of the ghastly context of united, human rejection of God, was to come to the whole earth. The Abrahamic covenant was God's international, blessing-filled covenant designed to counteract, undermine, and eventually overcome the problem of sin.

God also vowed, "I will bless you, and make your name great" (12:2 NASB). Isn't that what Babel's builders wanted for themselves? God continued, "and so you shall be a blessing." By going forth from his country, culture, creed, and caste, he would be a blessing. "And I will bless those who bless you, and the one who curses you I will curse. And in you some of the families of a small part of the earth will be blessed!" (wording mine). I caught you if you didn't catch my erroneous citing of Scripture. The covenant was not to bless *some* of the families of a *small* portion of the earth. Salvation's hypertext in the context of human judgment was envisioned for *all* the families of the earth.

The unconditional Abrahamic covenant is repeated throughout Genesis.[5] When the Bible uses a passive form of the covenant blessing, it refers to God's activity in choosing Abraham, which will bring good to all the nations. When the reflexive form is used, Abraham will himself enjoy a world-wide reputation from YHWH's blessing of Abraham and his descendants. The apostle Paul in Galatians 3:8 chooses the passive form to relate the international covenant to the Lord Jesus, "The Scripture, foreseeing that God would justify the Gentiles by faith, preached the gospel beforehand to Abraham, saying, 'All the nations will be blessed in you'"

(NASB). Abraham is not chosen for himself, nor merely for the blessing of his descendants and the cursing of his enemies, but for the blessing of *all* the families of the earth—God's international vision! God created the nations (Gen. 1–11), so He is working to bless the nations through Abraham's selection (Gen. 12ff).

In fact, the nation of Israel was created through Abraham, a non-Jew, of the lineage of Arpachshad (Gen. 11:12 NASB). God reminds Jerusalem, "Your origin and your birth are from the land of the Canaanite, your father was an Amorite and your mother a Hittite" (Ezek. 16:3 NASB). Israel was to confess that Abraham was "a wandering Aramean" (Deut. 26:5). Abraham wasn't created out of the ground like Adam. He carried a history from the nations and therefore was meant for the nations. God created the nations, so He is working for the good of the nations through Abraham. God could have chosen any man to create any nation, but God in sovereign grace chose Abraham to create Israel, no ordinary nation (cf. Num. 23:9).

Why did God choose Abraham? To implement an international vision.[6]

MOSES TO SOLOMON: AN INTERNATIONAL NATION

God, the Creator of humanity and the ruler of the nations, circumscribed one nation through which to implement His vision. The race began with Abraham. The nation's identity, constitution, and liberation were shaped in Egypt, to be consummated through Moses. Israel's exodus from Egypt made God look great and His character well known.[7] Each of the plagues was set in the context of Egyptian religion and mythology, a divine demonstration of their impotence.

The international dimensions of Israel's existence are evident in their national charter at Sinai. Here Israel became a kingdom, but it was chartered to be a kingdom of priests and a holy nation (Exod. 19:6). It is quite remarkable that the whole nation was to be a kingdom of priests. If the whole nation was to be priests, the question arises, "A kingdom of priests carrying out their duties to whom?" To the rest of the nations, of course.[8] Moses intercedes with God for Israel on the basis of the nations who had "heard of Your fame" (Num. 14:15 NASB).[9] One time "foreigners" are included with "natives" and even called "the people of Israel" (Josh. 8:33). Really, Israel was never completely alone in the Promised Land.

Throughout this period from Moses to Solomon, there were powerful instances of an *international* calling for Israel. From Rahab's protection (Josh. 2:10–12), to Naaman the Syrian captain, to the second and fifth books of the Psalms, God's international vision shines in these passages of Scripture. David's prayer for the community can be summarized as: "God bless us, . . . so that the ends of the earth may know your salvation" (cf. Ps. 67:1–2). This clearly states the identity, responsibility, activity, and ministry of Israel in relation to God and the nations.

Israel understood the international vision, initially and occasionally. During the intertestamental period, they were still going to great lengths in making proselytes (cf. Matt. 23:15). Some conservative movements in Judaism today understand their internationality based on the Old Testament alone. You can even dial a toll-free number or visit Web sites to become a "Jew by choice." Bearing international salvation, passively and actively, coming and going, centrifugally and centripetally, was Israel's assigned role in implementing God's Vision for the earth.

SOLOMON TO MALACHI: AN
INTERNATIONAL VISION

God's gift of unsurpassed wisdom and discernment to Solomon (1 Kings 3:12; 4:29–31) was recognized by Hiram, the king of Tyre who blessed the Lord (1 Kings 5:7); the queen of Sheba who "heard about the fame of Solomon concerning the name of the LORD" (1 Kings 10:1 NASB); and by "all the kings of the earth" (2 Chron. 9:23). Solomon's theologically loaded temple dedication prayer (1 Kings 8:22–61) included the foreigner, "when he comes from a far country for Your name's sake (for they will hear of Your great name and Your mighty hand, and of Your outstretched arm); when he comes and prays toward this house, hear . . . and do according to all for which the foreigner calls to You, in order that all the peoples of the earth may know Your name" (vv. 41–43 NASB). The purpose of the temple clearly expressed God's vision for the peoples of the earth through Israel. Solomon's finale fleshes out God's Vision and Israel's commission, "so that all the peoples of the earth may know that the Lord is God; there is no one else" (v. 60 NASB).

Fast-forward to the prophets, who see in the future a world period of Messiah's international rule. Global history will be culminated by wiping out tears and death (Isa. 25:6–8), the reversal of the nature curse (Isa. 11:6–9), and an immersion of the earth into the knowledge of the Lord (Isa. 11:9). The nation of Israel loses its prominence among the nations until God is vindicated in Israel and sanctified before the nations (Ezek. 36:22–23). Isaiah, the Old Testament "international evangelist," speaks of the day that the nations will resort to the root of Jesse (Isa. 11:10), the One whom he foresees in chapters 7–9. The Servant will bring justice to the nations (42:1). God invites the nations: "Turn to Me and be saved, all the ends of the earth; for I am God, and there is no other" (45:22 NASB). Israel will recognize her "international" Messiah, the One they pierced (Zech. 12:10), as the nations are drawn to Him (Zech. 8:22–23), and as He speaks peace to the nations (Zech. 9:9–10). Ultimately, YHWH will be king over all the nations.

The prophets' commission was to remind Israel of her role toward the whole earth, focused on the international vision of God. One day God will make Israel "a light of the nations, so that My salvation may reach to the end of the earth" (Isa. 49:6 NASB; cf. 66:18–21). Daniel and his three Hebrew friends expressed to Nebuchadnezzar and Babylon a message that mirrored Joseph's earlier witness to Pharoah and Egypt (cf. Dan. 2, 3, 6; Gen. 40). This divine message was also echoed in Nehemiah's testimony to Ahasuerus and Persia (cf. Neh. 2:1–10), and the earlier slave girl's witness to Naaman and Syria (cf. 2 Kings 5:1–14). We could go to Hosea's play on names ("not my people, you are my people," Hos. 2:23), to God's exodus of the Philistines and Syrians (Amos 9:7), to God's plan for the nations (Mic. 4:1–7), to God's promise to all flesh (Joel 2:28–32). In the last book of the Old Testament, the Lord of Hosts declares, "For from the rising of the sun even to its setting, My name will be great among the nations, and in every place incense is going to be offered to My name, and a grain offering that is pure; for My name will be great among the nations" (Mal. 1:11 NASB).

Sadly, however, Israel failed to understand the implications of her salvation for the world. Even some prophets hesitated to take YHWH to the nations. For instance, God had to overcome Jonah's exclusionary, elitist stance toward Nineveh's salvation. Israel lost her Architect's orientation, her calling. The Israelites thought that God existed for their salvation alone.

Consequently, their nation became built backward! Israel suffered the consequences of turning her back on her mission and the world. God's vision for the nation was not their vision for themselves. As history marches on internationally, God marches on with His vision—internationally.

FIRST COMING TO THE SECOND COMING OF JESUS: AN INTERNATIONAL PRESENT

God eventually instituted a new (to us) program to accomplish His international vision. After He sent the prophets and servants, God finally sent His Son (Mark 12:6; Heb. 1:1–3), His one and only Son (John 3:16–17), the second and last Adam (Rom. 5; 1 Cor. 15), "in order that in Christ Jesus the blessing of Abraham might come to the Gentiles" (Gal. 3:14 NASB). The Gentiles of Paul's day would become our "nations" of today—everyone not spiritually benefiting in Abraham's lineage through the Lord Jesus. A global re-visioning, reiteration, and renewal of God's international vision arrived through Jesus, the international Savior.

At Jesus' birth, wise men from the East came to worship Him. During His life, He ministered to the Jews but also to the Syrophoenician woman, the Roman centurion, and the Samaritan woman. In His teaching about the end vision, in response to a Gentile soldier's great faith, Jesus clarified the future, "I say to you that many shall come from east and west, and recline at the table with Abraham, Isaac, and Jacob in the kingdom of heaven" (Matt. 8:11 NASB). In His death, Jesus was the Lamb of God who takes away the sin of the world (John 1:29). God loved the *world* (John 3:16). In John 4:42, the Samaritans climaxed their conversion with, "we have heard for ourselves and know that this One is indeed the Savior of the world." (NASB). "As the Father has sent me," Jesus said, "I am sending you" (John 20:21 NIV)—to carry out the type and focus of His ministry. His resurrection implicates us "to bring about the obedience of faith among all the Gentiles" (Rom. 1:4 NASB). In Jesus' commission to His followers, echoed five times in the New Testament, the ends of the earth are in view.[10] Jesus possessed, demonstrated, and commanded an international vision.

At the present time, Jesus' church remains the arbiter-implementer of the divine global vision. At her founding on the Day of Pentecost, the church began the reversal of the tragedy of Babel by international representation. In Acts 2:5 devout Jews from *every nation* (remember Babel's diffused nations) under heaven were present in Jerusalem. These would have been both "scattered Jews" as well as Gentiles who had embraced Judaism. Check the amazement in Acts 2:6 (NASB), "each one of them was hearing them speak in his own language" (compared with Babel's confused tongues). Acts 2:7 notes that Galileans were clearly speaking different languages! The observers remarked, "How is it that we each hear them in our own language to which we were born?" (v. 8 NASB; also read a list of the nations in vv. 9–11). "We hear them in our own tongues speaking of the mighty deeds of God" (v. 11 NASB). Verse 12 (NASB) describes the impact of the event with a statement like, "They all continued in amazement and great perplexity, saying to one another, 'What does this mean?'"

Allow me to tell you what the message of these Scriptures means:

God's desire, focus, and plan are oriented toward the nations—His saving vision.
Salvation is internationally oriented. In Acts 4:12, though

unlearned and unschooled in Jewish matters, the apostles proclaimed, "there is none other name under heaven given among men, whereby we must be saved" (KJV).

The apostle Paul, in preaching and practice, in explicit statement and theological underpinning, clearly reaches out to the *whole* world. Examine any of his epistles to see the goal of his life, the reason for the church, and the design of God's salvation to be the international presentation of Jesus. Since there is so much material, I will summarize Paul's enthusiastic compliance with the international vision found in just *one* of his pastoral epistles, the book of 1 Timothy. The aging apostle reminds his young apprentice of the following aspects of the gospel he had received:

- ➤ *An international incarnation:* Jesus came into the *world* to save sinners (1:15).

- ➤ *An international mediator:* Jesus is the exclusive mediator between God and all humans (2:5).

- ➤ *An international presentation:* Jesus was proclaimed among the nations and believed on in the world (3:16) because He is the international Savior (4:10).

- ➤ *An international mandate:* Paul swears that he was appointed a preacher and apostle as a teacher to the nations in faith and truth (2:7). Some of his last words read, "the Lord stood with me and strengthened me, so that through me the proclamation might be fully accomplished, and that all the Gentiles [nations] might hear" (2 Tim. 4:17 NASB).

Non-Pauline epistles assume interaction with the world, too, as they encourage the church to maintain its identity and theology. There is to be separation from worldliness (e.g.,

1 Pet. 2:9–11) but interaction with unbelievers (1 Pet. 2:12). Christians are to "sanctify Christ as Lord in your hearts, always being ready to make a defense to everyone who asks you to give an account for the hope that is in you, yet with gentleness and reverence" (1 Pet. 3:15 NASB). The church ought to "proclaim the excellencies of Him who has called you out of darkness into His marvelous light" (1 Pet. 2:9 NASB). James directs us to outwardly demonstrate our faith (James 2:14–20). In Hebrews, Christ is God's final revelation to humanity (1:1–2), is superior to all previous monotheistic beliefs, and has tasted death for everyone (2:9).

God's international vision is finally accomplished in the book of Revelation. "Behold, He is coming with the clouds, and every eye will see Him, even those who pierced Him; and all the tribes of the earth will mourn over Him" (1:7 NASB). This one "was slain, and purchased for God with Your blood men from every tribe and tongue and people and nation; . . . and they will reign upon the earth" (5:9–10 NASB, cf. Babel and Pentecost). In a final attempt to reach all humanity, an angel from midheaven brings "an eternal gospel to preach to those who live on the earth, and to every nation and tribe and tongue and people" (14:6 NASB). John, in the book of Revelation, sees Isaiah's vision accomplished (Isa. 66:23 and Rev. 15:4) and sends out a final invitation on behalf of the Spirit and the bride, "Let the one who is thirsty come; let the one who wishes take the water of life without cost" (22:17 NASB).

Our ultimate vision and purpose for existence is neither our own lives, nor our vocation, or our family. The Protestant Reformation emphasized our responsibilities to work with our hands and minds to provide for our families. However, we must go beyond "civil vocation and sustainment of life" and "emphasize the other side, in order to recover the wider horizon of the Kingdom of God" as it "advances with power throughout the world. Contrary to much Reformational and Protestant teaching, the Kingdom of God is not limited to honest work in one's civil vocation, and in providing for one's family."[11]

The Monty Python television series brings serious laughter to my kids. In one episode, a guide to Mt. Kilimanjaro is being interviewed by a potential mountain climber. Now this particular guide sees everything double, and he speaks of the two peaks of Mt. Kilimanjaro. Challenged by the tourist on his two-peak theory, the guide shuts one eye and acknowledges the presence of only one mountain peak. He immediately announces the need to put a search party together "to climb the second peak so they could find the people from the last expedition who were building a bridge between the two peaks!" You cannot escape God's single-eyed vision in the Bible. We'll spell it with a capital "V" hence. God's Vision is international salvation, offered to humanity without cost, but with one condition—sole trust in Jesus alone. Since that condition exists, you ought to pursue the fulfillment of an internationally oriented salvation Vision in your life as well.

If you are typical of many Christians today, you may be seeing double. Your mission competes with your vision as an equally important mountain peak, when in reality there should only be one to climb. If your day-to-day life and efforts are not leading toward the fulfillment of God's Vision as your vision, you're actually trying to climb two mountains simultaneously—a guaranteed failure in attempting the impossible. Either your mission or your vision is imaginary (perhaps both). And if you try to solve this dilemma by proposing to build a bridge from your mission to life's vision, you lose people, including yourself. It's okay to be two eyed, but it's not good to see double. You'll not only confuse your-self; you may lead others in useless expeditions.

How do we go on a single-eyed journey, a solo-sighted vision, climbing one mountain peak? How do we get other segments of our lives—personal, family, and work—to sub-scribe to that single-eyed visionary journey?

I invite you to move into the next section of personal response to the Vision of God in finding and doing His will for you.

A Theology of Guidance

In her book *Staying Found: The Complete Map and Compass Handbook,* June Fleming suggests various ways hikers can master the skills of wilderness route finding—learning how to get around in the wild. By this, the author means, "Not just *carrying* a map and compass because they're on every book's list of essential items, but being *absolutely sure* of how to use them to fullest advantage. . . . Many hikers don't know *how* to stay found and, once lost, unwittingly compound their problems and work against being rescued."[1]

> The life that is committed
> to God has
> > nothing to lose,
> > nothing to fear,
> > nothing to regret.
>
> ✂ PANDITA RAMABAI

In this chapter, we will pursue how you can stay found for the rest of your life. You will need to use a spiritual compass, learning how to become a more skilled route *finder.* Not a route planner so much at first but a route finder. Fleming notes, "When searchers eventually locate lost hikers, alive or dead, they sometimes have with them compasses they never learned to use."[2]

Since you already possess a compass you can use, you will grow in way-finding skills as your confidence in the map Maker grows, even if you stray beyond the well-worn paths. In the next few pages, we will discuss a theology of personal purpose with special reference to divine guidance. We will primarily speak about the God of purpose and how the purposeful person lives under and looks for God's purpose, presence, and guidance in personal life. If you do this, you will stay found.

DIVINE PURPOSE

That the Creator has designed you on purpose shouldn't surprise you. A divine Creator without a supreme purpose cannot be worshiped, let alone loved, obeyed, and recommended. In spite of his own groundbreaking and mind-bending work in the field of quantum mechanics, Einstein refused to believe that "God plays dice with the universe."[3] A God of purpose reverberates all through Scripture; He created human beings purposefully to accomplish His purpose(s). God doesn't live by the seat of His pants in all sorts of powerful but arbitrary, clever but erratic ways. As *the* ultimate, omnipotent, strategic Planner, the omniscient Master Designer, the Chairman of the Board of the Universe, He cannot be characterized as a God of accidents. All history is made up of incidents, though they are not incidental to His purpose. Everyone, everything, everywhere lodges in His purpose for a purpose. He is the only One who doesn't die the death of a well-planned life. The Bible is explicit and articulate on the God of purpose and on God's purpose.

God has a purpose for creation and has made everything for a purpose.

God has a "plan of him who works out everything in conformity with the purpose of his will" (Eph. 1:11). "The LORD has made everything for its own purpose, even the wicked for the day of evil" (Prov. 16:4 NASB). This plan includes all of creation, salvation, time (past, present, and future), and reality at the minutest and largest levels.

God's purpose is settled, fixed, and unchangeable.

"He is mighty, and firm in his purpose," says Elihu (Job 36:5), an assertion that a plagued but defensive Job doesn't question but in fact confirms: "I know that you [God] can do all things; no plan of yours can be thwarted" (42:1). "For the LORD Almighty has purposed, and who can thwart him? His hand is stretched out, and who can turn it back?" (Isa. 14:27). Like His self-declared unchangeable nature (Mal. 3.6), God's purposes are unchangeable (Heb. 6:17). Neither time, people, nor circumstance can unsettle the purposes of God. "The plans of the LORD stand firm forever, the purposes of his heart through all generations" (Ps. 33:11). His purpose always prevails (Prov. 19:21). Jesus was handed over to be crucified by God's set purpose (Acts 2:23). Those who plotted the strategy, carried out the plan, and pounded the nails that killed Jesus only did what God's power allowed and what His will had decided beforehand would happen (Acts 4:28).

God never has to retract His purpose.

God never has to confess His ignorance or apologize for His thoughtlessness or admit His carelessness or acknowledge His intellectual weaknesses. These shortcomings, when attributed to God, reflect human limitations, including the tendency to think of Him in human terms. In His revealed purposes God is not unpredictable, though He is unfathomable. There are no holes in His administration, no gaps in His governing, and no delays in His execution. Human decisions must wisely change in real time as new information becomes available and new factors are taken into account. God instead proclaims, "I have decided and will not turn back" (Jer. 4:28). His omniscience guarantees an unchangeability of purpose.[4]

God moves human beings, even His enemies, to freely accomplish His purpose.[5]

Unbelievers are not privy to God's purpose or guidance unless He decides to reveal it to them (cf. Nebuchadnezzar in Dan. 2ff.; Cyrus in Isa. 45ff.). "Woe to those . . . who say 'Let God hurry, let him hasten his work so we may see it. Let it approach, let the plan of the Holy One of Israel come, so we may know it'" (Isa. 5:19). The single superpower leader of his time, Pharaoh was informed of God's particular purpose for him, displaying God's power and thereby declaring His name throughout the whole earth (Exod. 9:16; cf. Rom. 9:17).

God will bring all His purposes to pass.

He is pleased with His purposes: "I make known the end from the beginning, from ancient times, what is still to come. I say: My purpose will stand, and I will do all that I please" (Isa. 46:10). His children don't have to be afraid, however, for His purposes are based on His faithfulness to us: "O LORD, You are my God; I will exalt you and praise your name, for in perfect faithfulness you have done marvelous things, things planned long ago" (Isa. 25:1). His Word will accomplish His purposes: "So is my word that goes out from my mouth: It will not return to me empty, but will accomplish what I desire and achieve the purpose for which I sent it" (Isa. 55:11).

Sadly, it is possible to personally reject God's intentions *for you,* without sabotaging God's unchangeable purpose for you or the universe. Of course, this disobedience is understood in the "soft" sense that "you may decline His wishes for you." Jesus says, "The Pharisees and experts in the law rejected God's purpose for themselves, because they had not been baptized by John" (Luke 7:30). God "is patient with you, not wanting anyone to perish, but everyone to come to repentance" (2 Pet. 3:9), but those who do not believe on His only begotten Son will perish (John 3:16–18). His will for you is immutable, though His wishes for you may be refused.

The church, a new, post-Cross creation on earth, is as old as God's purpose, "but not made known to men in other generations" as now (Eph. 3:1–6). "By abolishing in his flesh the law with its commandments and regulations. His purpose was to create in himself one new man out of the two, thus making peace" (Eph. 2:15), a mystery not known in earlier generations. If you are a believer in the Lord Christ, you are part of His Pentecost establishment—the church, His eternal purpose newly revealed to the world in this time of His kingdom rule.

I close this section with the Suffering Servant's diatribe against the gods of Babylon, which explores many dimensions of the God of purpose:

> *Remember this, fix it in mind,*
>
> *take it to heart, you rebels.*
>
> *Remember the former things, those of long ago;*
>
> *I am God, and there is no other;*
>
> *I am God, and there is none like me.*

I make known the end from the beginning,

from ancient times, what is still to come.

I say: My purpose will stand,

and I will do all that I please.

From the east I summon a bird of prey;

from a far-off land, a man to fulfill my purpose.

What I have said, that will I bring about;

what I have planned, that will I do. (Isaiah 46:8–11)

PERSONAL PURPOSE

Everything in Scripture points to the ultimate purpose of God as being accomplished by real divine-human interaction. God uses our free intentions, choices, and actions to accomplish His *eternal* purposes *and* to fulfill His *unique* purpose for individuals. The psalmist declares both an assertion and a prayer, "The LORD will fulfill his purpose for me; your love, O LORD, endures forever—do not abandon the works of your hands" (Ps. 138:8).

Immediately following that confident personal declaration, Psalm 139 offers a most emphatic chapter on particular, distinct, and specific purpose for individuals, crafted by an all-present, all-knowing, all-powerful God. Open your Bible and follow along as we welcome the truths of Psalm 139.

Our connection with the psalmist emerges from correlating his individual existence and spiritual experience to our lives, rather than from his unique role as Israel's king. God not only knows, understands, and searches everything in general or in composite terms when it comes to David, the king of Israel; He also knows, understands, leads, and searches *you* and *me*.

God possesses *immediate* awareness of me. His knowledge includes *all* time—past, present, and future; *all* space—near and far, here and there, now and always, on land or sea, in the sky or in Sheol, in light or darkness (vv. 1–12); and *all* events in time and space—from birth to death and beyond (vv. 13–18). God doesn't need or possess secondhand knowledge of me. He knows me fully, immediately, and intuitively. His knowledge of me is not mediated, interpreted, or filtered through anyone else's eyes. When it comes to me, His full knowledge and real presence are critically contiguous. He knows me because He is present with me, and He is present with me in spite of His knowledge of me.

God's knowledge is also *intimate*. He is intimately acquainted with all my ways (v. 3). He is very familiar with all that is happening to me before it happens to me, as it happens to me, and after it happens to me. "Before a word is on my tongue you know it completely, O LORD" (v. 4). The psalmist feels the comfort of being enclosed by God's knowledge and hand. "You hem me in—behind and before; you have laid your hand upon me" (v. 5). Divine enclosure may seem suffocating and stifling, but God is not an unloving, cold, distant lover. The psalmist expresses wonder, relaxation, and confidence in God's embracing, comprehensive, intimate knowledge: "Such knowledge is too wonderful for me, too lofty for me to attain" (v. 6).

God's precious and vast thoughts toward me (vv. 17–18) not only relate to His immediate awareness and intimate acquaintance with me. They also show the Creator's *intricate* design of my life. "For you created my inmost being; you knit me together in my mother's womb" (v. 13). I am an embroidery of God's attentive work, a showpiece, a cross-stitched and knit masterpiece. I am as much a work of His fingers as the stars we examined in *Soul Mission* (Book Two of this series). The psalmist goes on to say, "I was made in the secret place when I was woven together in the depths of the earth. . . . All the days ordained for me were written in your book before one of them came to be" (vv. 15–16).

Several implications flow from these stunning verses about God's penetration into personal life, from the time we were conceived in His thoughts, woven together in our mothers' wombs, and then delivered to the earth for a specific, divine purpose.

Personal Uniqueness

"I praise you because I am fearfully and wonderfully made" (v. 14) could also be translated, "I am awesomely distinct."[6] You are an original, trademarked by God Himself. No imitator will succeed. You will not flatter anyone else by imitating them either.

Current scientific discussion on "distinctness of identity" comes to the fore in biotechnology's sequencing of every molecule in the human body. Unraveling the secrets of the DNA molecular structure provides quite the compliment to the Creator-Designer of the human body as scientists find out that life is more than locating individual genes in sequence. "The whole is greater than the parts, even as language is more than words in a dictionary."[7] As theoretical biologists understand how genetic components interact, how the environment influences organisms, and how nongenetic forces impact human development, they are thrilled with the startling confirmation of individual uniqueness.

Their studies corroborate the Scriptures. You are unique. There are no two people alike, even though they share genetic similarities with other humans and subhuman species. You are awesomely distinct. Even if they succeed in cloning part of you into one "like" you, there is only one "you." Each person is a work of art, or we might say, a fine example of "crafts-God-ship."[8] I am a unique design—a witness to the grand Designer who has imparted His identifiable company logo, the imprint of His image in my nonduplicable, non-replicable life. To state the obvious, you are unique, like the other six billion plus people presently on the planet!

Individual Purpose

"All the days ordained for me were written in your book before one of them came to be" (Ps. 139:16). The metaphor of the divine "book" is drawn from a Middle Eastern regis-ter containing the king's decisions for his subjects. Here the eternal One maintains a royal register of His decisions for your life. The Old Testament uses the "book" simile quite often in describing God's awareness and interaction with human life. Our tears are cataloged in His book, or scroll (Ps. 56:8). Our transgression record will and must be blotted out from His book (Ps. 51:1). Indeed, God's papyrus scroll con-tains and maintains a comprehensive record of the earth, its inhabitants, activities, and wrongdoing.[9]

Within this comprehensive record of all humanity is a record of my personal life. Not only does God know by divine omniscience how long you are going to live; He has planned out your details with divine care from the womb onward.[10] Affirming individual purpose allows God's omniscience to include you as more than merely instrumental within His pur-pose. God's prodigious genius uses you as "instrumental" in accomplishing divine purpose without diminishing you as an "end" in personal purpose.[11] God possesses a book, perhaps just a chapter—His own *sine qua non* book—on each one of us, a divine narrative on each human being. His handwriting is often illegible to us, easier read backward, and discernible only in general outline for the future. Having grasped this marvelous understanding of God's involvement from the time of our conception, the psalmist concludes, "How precious to me are your *thoughts,* O God!" (v. 17). The word thoughts can also be translated as "purposes" or "plans."

God's purposes for me are precious, but more important, His purposes are precious to me. I want to discern, nurture, and implement them.

His intentions are precious *toward* me. I will pursue His purposes and plans by asking, listening, and submitting to His leadership in daily life.

God has precious intentions—a specific purpose, a unique role, and a wonderful span—for your life and my life.

Divine Guidance

"Even there Your hand shall lead me" (Ps. 139:10 NKJV). The psalmist assumes the leadership of God in every place, time, and circumstance of life. God's strategic leadership is the basis of His invitation to us to listen to Him (Ps. 81:13); to wait and follow His instruction. Since God shepherds His sheep (Ps. 23:1; cf. Isa. 49:10; 57:18; 58:11), the psalmist consistently and confidently prays for God's teaching, showing, supervising, correcting, and leading (Pss. 25:4; 90:12) in his life. He affirms God's guidance till the end of his life (Ps. 73:24). "For this God is our God for ever and ever; he will be our guide even to the end" (Ps. 48:14). God counsels him (Ps. 16:7) and shows him the path to life (v. 11).[12]

The psalmist explicitly seeks God's leadership in daily life, for all of life: "Let the morning bring me word of your unfailing love, for I have put my trust in you. Show me the way I should go, for to you I lift up my soul. Rescue me from my enemies, O LORD, for I hide myself in you. Teach me to do your will, for you are my God; may your good Spirit lead me on level ground" (Ps. 143:8–10).

The issue in the Psalms is not whether God acts, intervenes, communicates, and leads. On the contrary, it is we who create and face the problems in a theology of guidance by not yearning, inviting, waiting, nor listening to God in active friendship and hospitality.

Spiritual Relationship

We boast independence, distance from God, prefer personal control over our lives, and manufacture private purposes to pursue. In contrast, the psalmist is filled with awesome wonder (Ps. 139:6), overwhelming gratitude (v. 14), and personal vulnerability in front of the all-knowing, ever-present, omnipotent God.

David's final thrust examines his own loyalties before the Lord. Anxious thoughts concerning his loyalties, motivations, fears, and the future penetrate him. The God who knows and controls everything must probe his inner being to enable him to know himself and to guide him. Discernment from God enables the discovery of God's ways for him. He surrenders his life as an open book to the God who searches and knows (139:1, 23). He requests a spiritual audit to see if his ways align with God's eternal ways (v. 24), according to the eternal purpose of God for his life (v. 16).[13]

GOD'S PURPOSE
AND PERSONAL PURPOSE

If a God of purpose has put me on the earth for a purpose, how do I discern my purpose and live according to His vision? Let's lay out a theological grid for personal purpose under the God of purpose; for unless you are committed to the God of purpose, there is no point talking about God's purpose for your life.

The Bible says that God wants to "show. . .the unchangeableness of His purpose" (Heb. 6:17 NASB) to the heirs of what was promised to Abraham—that's us! In the paragraphs that follow, you will find four dimensions that connect God's purpose and the personal purpose of believers.

Salvation

God's elective purpose resulted in our salvation. "And those he predestined, he also called; those he called, he also justified; those he justified, he also glorified" (Rom. 8:30). Our salvation fits His eternal purpose and results in the praise of His glory (Eph. 1:11–12). God saved us for a future heaven and has given us a guaranteed deposit for that purpose (2 Cor. 5:5–6).

Sanctification

God's purpose is our holiness, our sanctification. "For God did not call us to be impure, but to live a holy life" (1 Thess. 4:7). Sanctification is the outworking, the overflow of the realities of our salvation.

Suffering

A large part of Peter's first epistle is dedicated to how we suffer in God's will. We are neither to romantically embrace nor to run away from unavoidable suffering. Obeying God may entail suffering. So we are to suffer patiently, "for you have been called for this purpose, since Christ also suffered for you, leaving you an example for you to follow in His steps" (1 Pet. 2:20–21 NASB; cf. 4:1). Suffering produces sanctification. Later we will see that suffering functions as an index to discovering visionary service.

Service

The Lord Jesus was especially aware of His unique purpose on the earth.[14] He declared (Luke 4:18–19) and stuck to His purpose, "I must preach the good news of the kingdom of God to the other towns also, because that is why I was sent" (Luke 4:43). All through the Bible, God had special service purposes for individuals to fulfill, to carry out His ultimate purpose.[15]

While we list the above four divine purposes for Christians separately, like many aspects of biblical truth, they really comprise one package. Salvation, sanctification, suffering, and service are found together in 2 Timothy 1:9–12 (time and purpose emphasis added):

> [God] has **saved** us and **called** us to a holy life—not because of anything we have done but because of his own **purpose** and grace. This grace was given us in Christ Jesus **before the beginning of time,** but it has now been revealed through the appearing of our Savior, Christ Jesus, who has destroyed death and has brought life and immortality to light through the gospel. And of this gospel I was **appointed** a herald and an apostle and a teacher. That is why I am **suffering** as I am. Yet I am not ashamed, because I **know** whom I have **believed,** and am **convinced** that he is able to guard what I have **entrusted** to him **for that day.**

Salvation provides the premise for sanctification. God doesn't sanctify whom He has not saved, for salvation in itself is the first move of sanctification. God set you and me apart for Himself from the world to serve the world. Suffering is a significant instrument of ongoing sanctification in our lives. Suffering, in circumstance or by persecution, is permitted by God to conform us to His image and purposes.

God has also called us to unique and specific service toward His purposes. Too often, we actively pursue purposeful service before our appropriation of sanctification is in place or at least undergoing discernible process toward progress. Pragmatic in native constitution, driven to perform and yield results in business culture, our hectic service orientation precedes a passion for the reality of God in our lives. We need to beware of haste. Yet, there are others who are so oriented to *being* the right kind of inner person that they never go on to *doing* the right things. We need to beware of waste as well. Being right with God (theo)logically precedes doing right, but being right with God and doing right for God are integrally related in God's purposes for His children.

God, the omniscient Architect of the universe, patented the blueprint(s) for all reality. The blueprint is neither static nor passive, for He is also the omnipotent Architect. The active, dynamic blueprint as revealed in Scripture carries a theological tone. God's purpose reveals the salvation of humankind as its hypertext, the topline, the superstructure of God's program— His soteriological purpose. The subtext, the bottom line, the ground floor of God's entire planning and building process, is geared to make God look great—His doxological purpose. Since the doxological and soteriological purpose of God reflects God's agenda, we pray "thy will (or purpose)[16] be done in earth, as it is in heaven" (Matt. 6:10 KJV). If we belong to His global agenda—a purpose that comprises all reality, history, nations, church, and individuals—then we ought to discover and implement God's purpose for our lives.

When our purpose conflicts with His purpose, we learn to echo the words of the Lord Jesus, "Not my will, but yours be done" (Luke 22:42), and of David, "If it is the will of the LORD our God, . . ." (1 Chron. 13:2), and affirm James's caution, "If it is the Lord's will" (James 4:15), tomorrow we will do such and such. Our relationship to the purpose of God is one of adjustment, analogy, alignment. Jesus Himself sought to do the will of the One who sent Him (John 5:30) and delighted in it (Ps. 40:8). "In Luke 22:42, Jesus (with His 'if it be your will') appeals to the divine will, design and counsel, and makes Himself dependent on it at the very moment when the humanly anxious request for help and deliverances presses for utterance."[17] Similarly, we must do the will of God from the heart (Eph. 6:6). Since God's will is about Himself (doxological) and His salvation (soteriological), we simply subscribe to the divine blueprint and submit to the master Architect. Keep these aspects of God's will and purpose in mind as you discern God's direction for personal purpose in reorienting your life to His ultimate purpose in building life's superstructure.

Apparently God has a "wish" book (cf. 2 Pet. 3:9), a "will" book (Isa. 55:11); and a "without book" (Ps. 135:6; Eph. 1:9–11).[18] If you are presently included in the "without book," God can "equip you with everything good for doing his will, and may he work in us what is pleasing to him" (Heb. 13:21). Indeed, the one who does the will of God abides forever (1 John 2:17). I invite you to make God Himself the vision of your life and God's Vision your vision in life. Should you accept my invitation, you will never have to regret, doubt, or fear living the Intentional Life.

Sighting God's Guidance

During preparations for a road trip from Dallas, Texas, to Orlando, Florida, my brother dissuaded me from bringing our trusty Rand McNally road atlas. I like to see the entire route mapped on one or two pages—the states, the towns, the distances, the time it takes at speed limit. Instead, he wanted me to experience his new Global Positioning System. The annoying digital voice frequently announces turning directions and, as needed, recalculates the route. A beautiful color screen unfolds the way as we travel. Between

> *God gives to every man the virtue, temper, understanding, and taste that lifts him into life and lets him fall just in the niche he was ordained to fall.*
>
> — WILLIAM COWPER

sight and sound, we should make good time (especially since my brother's right foot is not yet spiritually mature). He's terribly dependent on the gadget for all his navigational needs.

The GPS works when a receiver on the ground calculates its position using time signals from the satellites and the high school math technique of triangulation to produce highly accurate coordinates of latitude and longitude. The GPS receiver works with map programs that monitor the vehicle's speed and direction, constantly updating longitude and latitude, and thus it always knows where we are. He just enters the destination and then leaves the driving, well, leaves the directing, to it. If we stop, the map stops. If we move away from it, whether accidentally or deliberately, the device continues to recalibrate to remind us that we are off course. As we move, the map unfolds right before us.

God's guidance fits the GPS model better than the paper map method. Its active, dynamic, real-time, as-you-go companionship suggests clear spiritual parallels. In pursuing *Soul Vision,* we program the destination—God's ultimate Vision. Then, as we move along God's course, our life map unfolds. Over the next chapters, we'll consider the biblical and practical aspects of discerning and going God's direction. How do we plan and move toward God's Vision? How do we find and live out His personal purpose for our lives?

PLANNING AND
THE ULTIMATE PURPOSE

We can know God's ultimate purpose from Scripture, and we will consider our unique purpose soon. Yet an intermediate question remains: *How may we resolve the significant issue of compatibility between God's ultimate purpose and our personal plans?* Again, the spiritual life is the key that opens this lock—the reason we began this examination of the Intentional Life with the subject of passion. Our confidence in God's providential control and our trust in His ongoing counsel enable us to know and obey His priorities in personal situations. His plan for us is accomplished as we fulfill His priorities and preferences in any given situation. It progressively unfolds as we simply obey, rather than insisting that God tell us His plans ahead of time so we can decide whether or not to obey.

God's *plans* are gleaned in the process of submission to the Holy Spirit, who has arranged life from the beginning, who is present in and with us all the time, and who leads us in His eternal purposes. God's *purpose* can be learned from studying Scripture, our world, and ourselves. We can know His purpose for us. It is foundational to our existence, woven into the fabric of our lives—past, present, and future. We will live out His plans in personal mission and fulfill His *purposes* in personal vision as we submit to the Lord's leadership.

Living out God's plans in accordance with His purpose develops as we listen to His instruction and counsel, and as we walk *daily* in His ways—personal mission. Moses already knew God's Vision for his life—to lead God's people (Exod. 33:12)—but he asked for God's favor in teaching him His ways in order to continue to find favor with God (Exod. 33:13). Moses realized God's unshakeable Vision was neither a basis nor an excuse for pursuing his own ends. God gave the psalmist ongoing counsel and instruction at night (Ps. 16:7) and broadened the path beneath him to keep him from slipping (Ps. 18:36). The condition for ongoing instruction in living out God's plans is an active, dynamic relationship to Him: "Who, then, is the man that fears the LORD? He will instruct him in the way chosen for him" (Ps. 25:12).[1] While there is debate on the promise of instruction in Psalm 32:8,[2] there is none on Psalm 73:24: "You guide me with your counsel." The psalmist prays to God, "Teach me your way, O LORD, and I will walk in your truth; give me an undivided heart, that I may fear your name" (Ps. 86:11). Later he prays, "Show me the way I should go, for to you I lift up my soul" (Ps. 143:8).

The verses and pages above have allowed us to review the theological underpinnings of divine purpose and personal purpose. We now go on to how we can purposefully live out

God's purposes. Two issues surface—the role of planning and the way of guidance. Let's put several biblical themes together to assist us in planning to live out God's purposes under His ongoing leadership.

First, we don't know the future, but God knows, controls, and directs the future. "The king's heart is in the hand of the LORD; he directs it like a watercourse wherever he pleases" (Prov. 21:1). "In his heart a man plans his course, but the LORD determines his steps" (Prov. 16:9). We can't boast about tomorrow (Prov. 27:1). There is no guarantee that tomorrow will be like today (cf. Isa. 56:12). Our fundamental limitation of not knowing what tomorrow brings accents the need for God's comprehensive involvement and consistent interaction in our lives. The only thing we know about the future is that God's purpose will succeed. "Many are the plans in a man's heart, but it is the LORD's purpose that prevails" (Prov. 19:21). Again, at last report, there is only One who can pledge the future.

Second, we can plan but we can't predict. To predict is to be presumptuous. Presumptuous planning exhibits a prideful independence and evidences sinful, human traits rooted near the beginning of time. At Babel, we saw a humanity confident of completing a project contrary to God's ultimate purpose, which would go unfinished. Jesus spoke of the rich fool planning to build bigger barns for greater storage yet not knowing the curtain was to drop on his life that very night (Luke 12:18). Jeremiah humbly declared, "I know, O LORD, that a man's life is not his own; it is not for man to direct his steps" (Jer. 10:23). A critical answer to our ignorance concerning a good future is God's stated purpose and program. If the Lord's purpose will prevail, our unique purpose might as well align with His ultimate purpose. Presumption will not succeed (see Num. 14:41–45).

Third, we can plan in the course of pursuing God's purpose for our daily lives. That's why we set objectives and goals. But we cannot direct our steps. We can't presume upon the future. We can't assume tomorrow's existence. But we can plan and must plan because the Scriptures tell us it is wise to plan. James chides us, not for planning but for thinking we can count on tomorrow for our plans (4:13). Instead, we "ought to say, 'If it is the Lord's will, we will live and do this or that'" (James 4:15). Planning that yields to God's will, that anticipates His direction, and invites His leadership is the most appropriate way to approach the future. We ought to ask the question of God's will with a will of submission. If God's will is pleasant, we submit. If it is unpleasant, we still submit. Facing the dastardly darkness of Gethsemane, the Lord Jesus submitted to the Father, "not what I will, but what you will" (Mark 14:36). Yet like the psalmist's desire to do God's will (Ps. 40:8), Jesus revels in God's will for Him: "I have come to do your will, O God" (Heb. 10:7).[3] The appropriate response to God's will for personal life is intense pursuit and consensual submission to God's plan, for even the wicked will fulfill His purpose. Revelation 17:17 brings God's purpose and human activity in balance: "For God has put a plan into their minds, a plan that will carry out his purposes" (NLT). Hence, I call for "open planning" or "submissive planning" that acknowledges God's purpose and our planning activity.

It is wise to plan, but plans must be committed to the Lord (Prov. 16:3) for blessing and fruition. Plans are not certain in their accomplishment, but they may be certified by the Lord. Whenever our plans come to pass, it is because He has approved, blessed, and completed them. "All that we have accomplished you have done for us," exudes Isaiah in praise

(26:12). Planning is expected of wise people in connection with other wise people (Prov. 15:22). "Make plans by seeking advice; if you wage war, obtain guidance" (Prov. 20:18). In the context of discipleship, Jesus encouraged forethought: "Suppose one of you wants to build a tower. Will he not first sit down and estimate the cost to see if he has enough money to complete it? For if he lays the foundation and is not able to finish it, everyone who sees it will ridicule him, saying, 'This fellow began to build and was not able to finish'"(Luke 14:28–30). Planning is discerning forethought (not foresight) accompanied by a mindset of submission. In humility and acknowledgment of God, we plan for this life (cf. Prov. 6:8, the ant that stores and gathers) and eternity itself (Luke 12:33).

So we are to plan, or better yet, to live out God's purpose for our lives with our plans committed and submitted to Him.

ACCESSING GOD'S GUIDANCE

Without equivocation, we declare that we need guidance and that God personally guides us. Guidance is part of His nature, a function of His position, and an overflow of His attributes of compassion and care. He leads and guides us for the sake of His name (Ps. 31:3). We don't worship a deistic God who acts in creation and salvation and then leaves us to our ingenious machinations or frantic guessing to work out His purpose in our lives. That God guides is neither hallucinating nor expressing what we hope will be the case. His ongoing guidance is indeed what God promises concerning Himself in relation to His people.

Some people propose discerning God's guidance based solely on scriptural precedents.[4] However, scriptural precedents don't necessarily *guarantee* present guidance for God's people. They only point to the fact that God can guide and that God has guided His people in the past. Consequently, we don't argue for God's ongoing guidance so much from prophetic or apostolic precedent. The theological issue is how we today enter into those biblical stories of yesterday. For instance, we have seen clear Scriptures about the nature of God as Savior and guide in relation to human spiritual needs for salvation and guidance. Divine nature is an unchangeable given, a cosmological constant through the ages, both in and outside the pages of Scripture. God's nature, role, and function are to guide His people. "He guides the humble in what is right and teaches them his way" (Ps. 25:9). He has not only guided in the past (biblical precedent); He is the God of ongoing guidance: "The LORD will guide you always" (Isa. 58:11). The extrapolated pattern of guidance is based on God's *nature* as guide, not just from His past *actions* as guide.[5]

Many problems on accessing God's guidance lie in our expectations of specificity, precision, and detail. A decision that seems trivial to some people paralyzes others, while what seems monumental to others feels like child's play to the mature. Again, much ink is spilt on what seems to be a rather straightforward promise: God provides guidance as we keep in concert with the Word and the Holy Spirit. Throughout history, Christians have aimed to affirm, connect, and submit to the leadership of the Word *and* the Spirit. What is unscriptural is simply not permitted in life. We do not have to ask God for guidance on that which is scripturally prohibited. However, there is immense latitude in decisions within the permissions of Scripture. It is in the narrow here and specific now that the Holy Spirit excels in providing illumination, priority, and specificity of direction for life.

The Word teaches us about the Spirit's role in life, and the Spirit teaches us about the Word's role in life. Most life decisions carry practical, moral, and ethical dimensions to them. Just as ethics without theology is deadly, theology without ethics can be dead, personally and to those around us. The Word provides the parameters within which we are to live. A great deal of freedom exists inside the direction of the Word. Within the Word's boundaries, the Spirit personally guides in the application of the Word to our unique and specific situations, if He is sought and if indeed guidance is necessary. For instance, the critical difference between dreaming the possible and the impossible comes from the leadership of the Holy Spirit inside the prescriptions and principles of Scripture.

SCRIPTURE AND SPIRIT

Let's look at God's guidance combining the Bible's and the Holy Spirit's continuous and active influence on our lives.

God teaches us by His Word; the Word gives moral and personal guidance. Psalm 119 superbly describes the brilliance of the Word in relation to guidance and direction. I have chosen a few verses and phrases from this magnificent treatment of God's Word as the path to enlightenment in daily life:

> ➤ "Blessed are they . . . who walk according to the law of the LORD," who "keep his statutes and seek him with all their heart" (vv. 1–2).

> ➤ God has "laid down precepts that are to be fully obeyed" (v. 4).

> ➤ "I have chosen the way of truth; I have set my heart on your laws" (v. 30).

> ➤ "Preserve my life according to your word" (vv. 37b, 40b, 50b, 93b, 107, 149b, 154, 156).

➤ "I will always obey your law, for ever and ever" (v. 44).

➤ "This has been my practice: I obey your precepts" (v. 56).

➤ "Teach me knowledge and good judgment, for I believe in your commands" (v. 66).

➤ "Before I was afflicted I went astray, but now I obey your word" (v. 67, cf. v. 71).

➤ "I have put my hope in your word" (vv. 74b, 81b, 114b, 147b).

➤ "I have more insight than all my teachers, for I meditate on your statutes" (v. 99).

➤ "Your word is a lamp to my feet and a light for my path" (v. 105).

➤ "I am your servant; give me discernment that I may understand your statutes" (v. 125).

➤ "Direct my footsteps according to your word; let no sin rule over me" (v. 133).

God's Word, then, is fully adequate for guidance during our times of clarity and at our points of confusion. Never exceed the bounds of His Word, particularly when you are unsure as to what you should do. To exceed the boundaries causes further tension, cacophony, and befuddlement. Within the bounds of His Word, there may be many options. Live in the freedom of the Word. If you seek specific direction, make your requests known to God, who guides with and from the Word in applying truth practically in order to provide His presence and guidance.

To illustrate, the Bible is the compass even as the Holy Spirit is the Captain-Guide—everything we need for direction can be found with compass and guide. Normative revelation—the Bible— tells us the *what* of His purposes; personal revelation by the Holy Spirit tells us the *how* of His purposes for us within biblical criteria. The Bible points us in the direction; the Holy Spirit leads, sustains, empowers, and befriends us on the journey. Human limitations keep us from possessing an entire road map. All we can know is if we are headed on roads that have been traversed before toward God and His ultimate purpose. This knowledge draws out our personal purpose and drives the will. If we have been keeping notes in and on the past, we possess solid understanding on where we have been. We are rather aware of where we are at present, but we don't know what tomorrow will bring.

In the middle of the dreary Pilanesburg Game Reserve in South Africa, Temba served as our guide for the game drive. As the evening wore on, it turned cold for those who thoughtlessly took only summer clothes to the Southern Hemisphere. After sighting the Big 4 of the Big 5 (elephant, leopard, lion, and rhino—we missed the water buffalo), we were ready to go back to the rooms. Except, we weren't sure where we were. Even the signposts beside the dusty roads that proclaimed unfamiliar options, destinations, and distances didn't make sense to us. But our confidence in Temba, our guide, and the reliability of the signs, though unfamiliar, gave us confidence in the dark, in the wild, in the unknown.

In the same way, the Bible provides us with reliable signposts and the Holy Spirit is our dependable guide in the dark. We travel on roads that have been used before, and our divine Host-Guide assures us of eventually reaching His/our common destination.

If we need to demarcate them in the Bible, we find *human* (e.g., in the psalmists' assertions) and *divine* statements about God's presence, leadership, and companionship. The supposedly "human statements" may be dismissed as wish projections or spiritual desires expressed about God. While spotting this distinction between human and divine statements about God is not usually difficult in Scripture, we clearly see God's assertions on guiding, helping, caring, and companionship. His statements in Isaiah's Servant Songs apply to us as individuals led by the guiding, sustaining God:

➤ "So do not fear, for I am with you; do not be dismayed, for I am your God. I will strengthen you and help you; I will uphold you with my righteous right hand" (Isa. 41:10).

➤ "I will lead the blind by ways they have not known, along unfamiliar paths I will guide them; I will turn the darkness into light before them and make the rough places smooth. These are the things I will do; I will not forsake them" (Isa. 42:16).

➤ "This is what the LORD says—your Redeemer, the Holy One of Israel: I am the LORD your God, who teaches you what is best for you, who directs you in the way you should go" (Isa. 48:17).

➤ And to those who obey the Great Commission, Jesus promises, "I am with you always, to the very end of the age" (Matt. 28:20).

When we became believers, divine Presence took residence in us. The Holy Spirit became a permanent indweller in me at salvation. Paul unequivocally declares, "God's Spirit lives in you" (1 Cor. 3:16), "your body is a temple of the Holy Spirit, who is in you" (1 Cor. 6:19), and "the Holy Spirit who lives in us" (2 Tim. 1:14). Divine Presence, then, is not only a motivation for staying morally pure and guarding salvation truth; it is also God's way of leading us in truth—in true conviction and obedience (1 John 2:27).[6]

Unfortunately, many Christians affirm God's omnipresence but not His active indwelling and companionship. God does not resemble one's parents. When I left my parents and moved ten thousand miles away, they came along with me, passively, in teaching and in memory. Their active presence was a past thing. They were not with me in immediate conversation and friendship, in the here and now. God's presence, however, is not merely in teaching and memory. He is not only active in past history but operates in present time, real time. He is presently present inside me, in active companionship, in a fellowship of kindred spirits. His Word—outside of me—is presently true for my life. His Spirit—inside me—presently guides my life.

With God's Word and His Spirit in, around, above, under, and before me, I depend on His ongoing guidance, even as I count on His permanent presence (Heb. 13:5). God's presence and guidance are critically connected. This is not simply a "background presence," like some religions teach about the Divine Spirit, the Good Lord, the Great Being in the sky. God is actively present in you and is your faithful companion. He is not only there to lift you up when you fall; He is there to prevent your falls. His presence, though invisible, is not passive. Guidance arises from a dynamic companionship with almighty God as you interact with Him. Through our knowledge of God and His Word we have "everything we need for life and godliness" (2 Pet. 1:3).

Like the two blades of a scissor, the Bible and the Holy Spirit cut through the obstacles and make way for our future in the present.[7] The Bible points the way, provides the guide-

lines, and furnishes the prescriptions for daily living. The Holy
Spirit helps, comforts, teaches, and guides us inside the parameters, boundaries, and demands of the Word from the present.

The psalmist knew that guidance was found in the teaching and leadership of the Holy Spirit. He prayed, "Teach me
to do your will, for you are my God; may your good Spirit
lead me on level ground" (Ps. 143:10). The Holy Spirit is
called the "Spirit of counsel" (Isa. 11:2), for He has always
been in the business of instruction (Neh. 9:20). What the
psalmist knew in a limited way is possible and true for us by
the fuller revelation and special salvation status we have
received with God. The Lord Jesus promises us the full provision of the Holy Spirit: "If you then, though you are evil,
know how to give good gifts to your children, how much
more will your Father in heaven give the Holy Spirit to those
who ask him!" (Luke 11:13). That incredible promise comes
to us in the context where Jesus speaks of "asking, seeking,
and knocking" (v. 9).

God's purpose for me and my purposeful living for Him
is an interaction of two dynamic factors in collaboration.
The first dynamic comes in the psalmist's prayer: "I cry out
to God Most High, to God, who fulfills his purpose for me"
(Ps. 57:2). This tells me that God's purpose for me will prevail. He fulfills His purpose for me. The second dynamic
comes from Paul, who tells us how it happens: "for it is God
who works in you to will and to act according to *his good
purpose*" (Phil. 2:13, emphasis added). Since God works in
me, I can will and act according to *His* good purpose.

Some of the most compelling lessons in God's Word flow
from Spirit-inspired metaphors for accessing personal guidance. Let me add biblical data on God's guiding leadership
from word pictures in the Scriptures.

The Lord as light (Ps. 27:1). He calls us from darkness into His light (1 Pet. 2:9). When a person falls, the Lord will be a light even though he sits in darkness (Mic. 7:8). He sheds light on the righteous (Ps. 97:11), throws light on the dark situation (Ps. 112:4), on our ways (Job 22:28), and turns our darkness to light (Ps. 18:28). Psalm 119:130 claims, "The unfolding of your words gives light." Read that verse again. We need the unfolded Word for light, unfolded by the Holy Spirit, of course. Light provides enlightenment in the present situation of darkness but also gives direction in future blankness. Zechariah affirms the coming of the messianic child as prophet of the Most High, "to give light to those who sit in darkness and the shadow of death, to guide our feet into the way of peace" (Luke 1:79 NKJV). Since the Lord is light, "the path of the righteous is like the first gleam of dawn, shining ever brighter till the full light of day" (Prov. 4:18).

The Lord as shepherd (Ps. 23:1). The chief (1 Pet. 5:4), the good (John 10:11), and the great (Heb. 13:20) Shepherd does what shepherds do—guides sheep. "He makes me lie down in green pastures, he leads me beside quiet waters" (Ps. 23:2). The chief Shepherd leads His people through under-shepherds (1 Pet. 5:1, 4; cf. the Shepherd of Israel theme in Pss. 77:20; 78:52; 80:1). Isaiah 40:11 reads, "He will feed His flock like a shepherd; He will gather the lambs with His arm, and carry them in His bosom, and gently lead those who are with young" (NKJV). The New Testament repeats the shepherding theme. The sheep hear the voice of the good shepherd: "He calls his own sheep by name and leads them out. When he has brought out all his own, he goes on ahead of them, and his sheep follow him because they know his voice" (John 10:3–4).

The Lord as mother eagle (Deut. 32:11–12). "Like an eagle stirs up its nest and hovers over its young, that spreads its wings to catch them and carries them on its pinions, the LORD alone *led* him" (emphasis added). This eagle-as-parent metaphor for God shows how His loving wisdom *leads* His people into difficult situations to strengthen and grow without forfeiting protection.

The Lord as path maker, path leader, and path straightener. The psalmist asks God to lead him in a straight, leveled path (Ps. 27:11). The straightening of paths (Prov. 3:6) shows God as director of our paths and the One who clears obstacles in those paths. He is a path maker, not having to be a pathfinder!

The Lord as a guiding hand. The Lord's *hand* shows goodness (2 Chron. 30:12), sustenance (Ps. 37:25), protection (John 10:28), discipline (Ps. 32:4; Acts 13:11), and care (Isa. 41:10). God's hand implicitly provides leadership in that care: "The gracious hand of his God" was on the leader and the people as Ezra (Ezra 7:9; cf. 8:18) and Nehemiah (2:18) led the exiles. God took them by the hand to lead them out of Egypt (Heb. 8:9). There is no place where His hand will not guide (Ps. 139:9–10), or where we can flee His presence or His hand of leadership (Ps. 139:7–8).

If you doubt that God personally guides, just ask around. Thousands of stories of God's personal guidance to believers can be found all around you. God goes to any length to give instruction, provide angles, furnish insight, and specify details to the person who desires to do His will. He will also guard you in your pursuit of His will. We do not need to fear what the future holds, for as the old line goes, we do know who holds the future. The nature of the Guide and Guard not only guaranteed the discovery of personal guidance before the New Testament was written, but also before it was translated in language understandable today. I can point to specific examples of *personal* revelation (not *normative* revelation by any means):

> to a Ukrainian Baptist pastor in finding a wife twenty years ago;

> by *circumstances* in helping a South African missionary to discern the specific vision of ministering in Botswana;

> by spiritual *counsel* for particular school decisions in my own life;

> by extraordinary and timely granting of Scripture— the unfolding of His Word—for decisions with large implications.

When I teach a course on "Shepherd Leadership" with an emphasis on strategic planning in various settings around the world, I notice a striking difference between my audiences. Steeped in business literature, my Western audiences point to "making goals" as the first step in planning. Arising from biblical premises and texts, non-Western audiences consistently point to prayer as the first step in planning. I am convinced of the godly wisdom in the non-Western first step in articulating this theology of personal guidance, and following through with the Western first step as the second step. This is not unlike Jehoshaphat's directive to the king of Israel, "*First* seek the counsel of the LORD" (1 Kings 22:5, emphasis added).

If we put divine companionship, divine leadership, and divine providence together, the conclusion of the matter is not difficult. If we follow biblical patterns, including the prescription of inquiring of God (e.g., 1 Chron. 14:14; Ps. 24:6), living in His calling (Eph. 4:1), and continuing in Him (Col. 2:6), the conclusion of the matter is plain. It is hard to miss out on God's guidance when you are interacting with God on any and every matter, when you are carrying out His will, or when you are looking for it. "Ponder the path of thy feet, and let all thy ways be established" (Prov. 4:26 KJV). We shall ask God to teach us His ways (Ps. 86:11; Mic. 4:2) as we walk by faith (2 Cor. 5:7) in the Son of God (Gal. 2:20).[8] Keep moving toward His ultimate purpose, and His spiritual GPS coordinates will lead you through the stoplights, traffic jams, shortcuts, detours, bypasses, and highways of life.

(handwritten notes:)
Jms. 1:5
- Seeking council of the Lord
- by Faith Heb. 11:6
- we) love
Hope 2 Tim 3:16
- Pray - philip. 4:6

Finding God's Will

6

(handwritten notes:)
Sis Evelyn Nube

Don't think about finding God's will but doing God's will!

We now come to questions that have frequented Christians over years of discussion. Does God have a unique purpose for individuals to fulfill? Does God have a specific plan for me to consummate, a straight line to which I must adhere, a narrow street on which I must travel? How will He reveal it to me? If He doesn't and I miss it, is all lost?

Should one focus on God's will in terms of which college to go to, which job to accept, which person to marry, which dress to wear, which toothpaste to buy? We can experience indecision, tension, and worry with these issues.

> *Expect great things from God;*
> *Attempt great things for God.*
>
> ❧ WILLIAM CAREY

Obviously, in a hierarchy of importance, finding a wife is more important than deciding what socks to wear, which route to take, or even which car to buy. It is only in *our* perception of the relative importance of somewhat plausible options that life becomes unnerving. Since many authors have considered the question of God's will at length through the lenses of Scripture, theology, history, and experience, I merely suggest the following abridgement.

THE ROLE OF FAITH
IN DISCOVERING GOD'S WILL

First, here is a theological grid to combine freedom and faith in finding personal guidance:

God defines the ends *of His will and gives you increasing freedom within it.* Take the clear statement of God's will for you to be "sanctified" (1 Thess. 4:3–4).[1] Sanctification is the end. So you go to the college, take the job, marry the person, wear the dress, and use the toothpaste that will not compromise your holiness. Depending on the level of maturity, you will apply that *end* to the right and pertinent issues. Some issues are not simply pertinent to that *end*. God defines the unmovable ends and gives you increasing responsibilities within them. Since you are a growing Christian, you actively consult the Compass (the Word) and your Captain-Indweller-Companion (the Holy Spirit) for pertinent ends on each and every situation.

God preserves you from unnecessary mistakes (cf. Acts 16:6). Looking backward, all your mistakes, moronic behaviors, and even past sins were inevitable ones. You will make mistakes in the future as well, inevitable as to kind (because nothing happens without God's will) but not as to sin (because God doesn't tempt you with evil). Insensible and insensitive Christians need to understand the will of the Lord (Eph. 5:17). The mature Christian keeps on pleasing God, thereby fulfilling His will.

God does not obligate Himself to telling you everything about the rest of your life. He has told you about the end of your life—to glorify God; and the afterlife—to be with Him forever. It is between the ultimate and the immediate—the intermediate zone—that we seek God's guidance. His expectations are clear. Live the rest of your life in concert with His

Word and Spirit, and by His will you will exploit the future for Him (cf. Rom. 15:32).

THE ROLE OF THE SPIRIT IN DISCERNING GOD'S WILL

Second, let's explore a theological summary of the Holy Spirit's leadership role in personal guidance.[2]

The Holy Spirit always leads within the bounds and boundaries, permissions and prohibitions, exhortations and principles of Scripture. Don't begin to look for guidance if your attitude toward Scripture is not one of humility and openness toward God. A friend who left his wife of thirty years and five children for his marketing assistant wrote me saying, "God has brought a significant other into my life." I asked him "which God?" Saying "I feel the peace of Christ in separating from my spouse" is wrong, even if you rationalize it with godly language. Study Scripture first. The Spirit's personal guidance may specify the application of God's truth in particular situations that go beyond Scripture, but it never will contradict it.

The Holy Spirit helps you to understand the relative importance of a decision and the amount of energy to be spent on it. Since you don't know when small decisions carry big ramifications, the Holy Spirit guides you in what decision you must invest your spiritual energy. I didn't spend much time thinking of which road to take to the office today, but I did spend some time reflecting on the role of the Holy Spirit in decision making to write this paragraph. He preferred that I spend more time on the latter. Occasionally, which road I take to the office may be more important than the latter, an issue that the Holy Spirit must help me sift through and choose. Sometimes, it is wiser for me to drive by the cemetery on a side road, because my busyness needs to be moderated by an awareness of life's frailty. The Holy Spirit superintends and strengthens us in understanding priorities in life that need His more intensive intrusion. The "gentleman" Holy Spirit does not hesitate in intruding and disturbing a heart humbly open to Him.

The Holy Spirit highlights appropriate Scripture to you. You may see passages in ways you've never seen them before. Sometime ago, I was struggling through a decision that would affect our ministry for the next ten years, wrestling over the tension between godly ambition and foolish presumption. I read the last verse of Colossians 1: "To this end I labor, struggling with all his energy, which so powerfully works in me." The word *His* jumped out and grabbed me, for whatever I decided, I would be laboring with all *His* energy! The Holy Spirit knew that on that fair fall day of October 23, 1998, I would be devotionally reading this verse and decided to provide me with additional encouragement to persevere in the decision.

The Holy Spirit reminds you of your values and their impact on your decision. Remember our treatment of the Beatitudes and the extravagant implications of each of those values in Book One, *Soul Passion*? Further, in Book Two, *Soul Mission,* we looked at financial stewardship and constructing the "without list." I shared my family considerations in buying a larger house in view of changes in family seasons, especially evident in our kids' new physical sizes! Our values included "merciful giving" and "no debt" so we can give without reservation. Merciful giving would be easier for us without borrowing money, even if borrowing money has been the cheapest it has ever been. We chose to remodel our home and make an extra room out of a larger one. God provided guidance for this decision in ways that are peculiar to Him—through a new "interior designer" friend who gives special rates to special friends, and a talented young man who would beat the market price for contractors, etc.

The Holy Spirit reinforces the virtues that He has worked in you in terms of a decision. You may recall the treatment in Book Two, *Soul Mission,* of the fruit of the Spirit as "virtues" that God brings to fruition in your life. When we learn to do life "by the Spirit" (Gal. 5:16–25), we will not only sublimate the flesh, but we will also be "led" by the Spirit. While fleshly acts are immoral, spiritual virtues are proof of His work. Think about a decision in terms of the fruit. For instance, how does love bear on an issue? Let's look at some trivial daily issues. Is it God's plan that you engage in personal hygiene when you could use those fifteen minutes to check your e-mail instead? Even if you need to make petty decisions about showers, shower today because you love your neighbor. For their sakes, please decide to shower! Should you get into an exercise program? The fruit of loving your family and being faithful to your calling applies to that decision. Should you eat a second helping of ice cream? How does that relate to the virtues of love, faithfulness, and self-control? Fruit creation and virtue reinforcement also enable the Spirit's control of your energies and reactions in thinking, planning, and implementing decisions. The power to apply values and virtues to every decision comes from keeping in step with the Spirit (Gal. 5:25), since you live by the leadership of the Spirit.

The Holy Spirit reveals implications of a decision ahead of time. Some implications do not need clarification, though reiteration becomes very important. Everybody knows "borrowing money makes the debtor a slave to the lender"—a scriptural principle illustrated by daily life. However, some implications are less obvious and need divine, personal revelation. "I knew before we were married that Ramesh would live a peripatetic preacher's life; he belonged to the world," says my wife now. Often. She never once said it while we were preparing for marriage. Who gave her the insight into the implications of marrying me (and grace to live with me since—it takes less grace to live with me when I am absent!) ahead of time? The Holy Spirit.

The Holy Spirit enables you to see angles of the decision that are not immediately evident. On my side of the story, the Holy Spirit explored the "Should I marry Bonnie?" question by enabling me to notice her father's lifestyle as a pastor. Bonnie was a person the Lord had already prepared for a ministry lifestyle—extended absence from family, frugal use of money, and appreciation of ministry. Watching her mother take care of her grandmother showed me their family's value toward older people—a distinct observation usually missed in blind romance.

The Holy Spirit probes your motivations, clarifies them, and helps you correct them if necessary. Again I will use the example of my wrestling with God regarding the future of our ministry. Should we use the first ten years of the new millennium (2000–2010) to evangelize one million opinion leaders and strengthen one million pastoral leaders? or one hundred thousand of each? One hundred thousand is no small number, but it is a pittance given the huge numbers of people that have not yet heard of Christ. One million seems unrealistic for our small organization. The larger number appealed to the audacious, bodacious side of me. The smaller number seemed more achievable. I had to check the motives on both sides of the question. Do I pursue the smaller number because of my desire to play it safe, take little risk, and say at the end of the period that we had done it? Or, do I pursue the larger number simply because some of our constituency would be thrilled with large numbers and would applaud the ministry? Both motivations reflect pride—so pride was not the issue. What decision will take *less* pride and less of self, given my tainted life, became the question.

The Holy Spirit creates the circumstances and brings alongside people who can have bearing on a particular decision. As part of His providential control, the Spirit allows people and circumstances to provide insight into a decision. Some time ago the brochure of an acquaintance's ministry arrived on my desk. It was sent by a friend, asking what I thought of this man's ministry as the cover blared his desire to train "one million pastoral leaders in two years." I liked the numerical goal—because that's what needs to be done, but I seriously doubted his capacity. I did not think that he nor I, nor both of us together, could pull it off. In ten years maybe, but not in two. Later, I providentially/accidentally ran into a friend at the airport with whom I was able to share our prospective ministry goal dilemma. He confirmed the one hundred thousand objective, saying "you can always revise the number up when you reach the one hundred thousand." I know both the smaller and greater numbers goals are important. So what credence do I give to the apparent "accidental" contact I made as related to the purpose that the Lord has for me?

Never use circumstances independently of godly counsel, however providential they seem to be. Circumstances without wise, interpretive counsel result in divination. Often the test of your commitment to a calling will exceed circumstances. Circumstances may serve to correct but not validate a decision. Use *individual* experiences as cautions but not as guidance for a decision. Only *patterns* of experiences may help confirm understanding toward a decision. Like any anecdotal proof, circumstances and experiences can be used in opposite ways of interpreting life.

The Holy Spirit reduces inner tensions and increases conviction toward a particular decision, by giving you faith tempered by wisdom, and the common sense accompanied by faith, to believe something is good and possible. We are not referring to positive thinking based on inner prowess but godly thinking growing out of love for Christ and a commitment to His glory. There is no difficulty in dreaming impossible dreams! Everyone wishes, imagines, dreams. We need to ask what possible dreams we should envision, by the mixture of faith and wisdom.

This aspect of the Spirit's role happened for me as I rode on my exercise bike, a few days after I had met my friend at the airport. I broke the tie between the one hundred thousand and the one million decision. We should strive to introduce one million opinion leaders to the gospel, by "every which wise and wide way" known to us, but cultivate the *responses* of one hundred thousand with a follow-through program. Provide one million pastoral leaders with tools indirectly, through a coalition of organizations, and one hundred thousand leaders with skills directly, through on-site training ministry. I am still echoing the words I repeated a half-dozen times in exhilaration, "You gave it to me, . . . You gave it to me." It wasn't *"Eureka!"* (Greek for "I found it!"), nor *"ah-ha"* (slanguage for "I understand it"), but *"edokas"* (Greek for "you gave it; you granted it!"). Hallelujah!

The strange fact of the matter is that we actually sense a need to expose one billion individuals to the Good News directly or through others for that "one million opinion leaders, one million pastoral leaders mandate" to be accomplished. The billion number has become our vision, and the million number is a mere means to the vision. God not only gave the direction but is presently granting the fulfillment of His direction. We now live humbly dependent on His provision to accomplish His vision through us.

The Holy Spirit possesses the prerogative to simply "hit" you with special guidance, but always within the bounds of Scripture. He could tell you to marry a certain person, pursue a certain vocation, buy a certain car, and serve in a certain ministry. I find that the less mature one is, the more he or she needs these "direct hits" of the Holy Spirit. The greater one's maturity, the more a person can discern these things from an active companionship with the ongoing leadership of the Holy Spirit, in conjunction with God's Word. Unfortunately, we often desire to exchange maturity for direct revelation—a mark of spiritual immaturity.

STEPS TO SEEKING GOD'S WILL

God's will for personal life cannot be missed if we are seeking His will. Face every decision on that basis. Move into the future, not paralyzed with whether or not you are doing God's will in a situation but seeking to please God in every known situation. We prefer to be eternal imbeciles not taking responsibility for a decision rather than acknowledging human limitations and making decisions with known factors, trusting Him to preserve us from unnecessary mistakes—as long as we are seeking to please Him. The disciplines of attachment, detachment, alignment, and engagement (discussed at length in Book One, *Soul Passion*) keep you in active consultation with the Word and the Holy Spirit. "First seek the counsel of the Lord," and then live in an ongoing manner by faith, in hope, and with love.

Make a list of all your present issues that need guidance—in personal, family, and work life. For my family, *present* issues relate to everything from today's luncheon speaking engagement, one child's poor report card, the other child's bug collection assignment, our daughter's basketball team try-outs, music lessons for all the kids, tonight's family time since I am gone for the weekend, repainting of our living room, to the college choice for our oldest, and so on. These numerous daily issues captivate my and your personal mission attention and values. Once you have identified these immediate issues, then pray! By the time this work is published and read, we will have already accomplished God's will in these areas and more.

How can you and I find the will of God in these issues? By acknowledging that the Christian life in the middle of the muddle is the will of God for my life. *Living the will of God in a biblical lifestyle and in dependence on the Holy Spirit is God's will for my life.* Now take the specific issues and do the following for guidance:

➤ Search the Bible for propositions and implications on the matter. (Does it matter which music teacher my daughter takes for keyboard lessons? Probably not. I have no direct Scripture teaching on the matter, though I would prefer a competent, effective Christian teacher to a nonbeliever, all other things remaining equal.)

➤ Pray deliberately about the matter. Ask God to surface issues of which you are unaware.

➤ In an attitude of prayer, think about (you can even

write out) the issues, both explicit and implicit, implications, and consequences on your life. Ask for wisdom in terms of the long-term. The discipline of writing it out will help you think clearly. On deeper or bigger decisions I usually do a two-columned "gains and losses" study. Similar to a "strengths, weaknesses, opportunities and threats" (SWOT) analysis, my "gains and losses" reflection considers two rows of *real* and *potential* angles under the "gains and losses." I also prayerfully seek God's leadership in order to attribute the right significance to each entry. When you do this study under God, you will discover new angles on the matter. You will also keep a record of God's faithfulness in leading you. Listen to God at this time.

➤ Make a decision, submit that decision to the Lord to receive, reject, or redefine it. If your decision doesn't correspondingly increase in conviction toward its accomplishment, be cautious. Wrestle thoughtfully with your decision, with an open heart and mind. Talk to mentors. Look for counselors and circumstances by which God can instruct you. Don't go forward unless you sense increasing certainty about it. Between scriptural parameters, circumstantial providence, and personal preparation, God leads clearly and simply. He does not confuse His children. When guidance takes longer than expected, your response is to wait for His simple, sober, and sure direction.

➤ Once the decision is made, settle it with conviction. Expect doubt, but don't be double minded about it. Decision making is a journey of faith, undergirded by faith, and continued in faith. Your confidence is in God, who can allow you to make a huge mistake and yet providentially correct it in the future.

➤ Finally, go forward with it. Humbly give God the right to overturn your decision or teach you in the middle of a bad decision, or give you ease of accomplishment in it.

The norm for the spiritual life lies in intentional dependence, conscious surrender, and prayerful conversation with the divine Indweller-Leader-Helper-Companion. You can't miss out on His guidance unless you intentionally reject it (cf. Jer. 32:33). We are too struck with finding God's will when we should be dismayed at not doing what we already know to be His will. God is under no obligation to reveal the unknown when we don't obey the known. However, when we combine God's permanent presence with God's ongoing instruction, there is no way we cannot access His guidance for our lives if we seek it, obey it, and look some more.

Like many other aspects of spiritual truth, guidance is always available and possible except when we rebel against the Guide or reject His counsel. One simply counts on the reality and availability of His guidance to move forward. He possesses the power and the will to intervene and stop you if you inadvertently waver from His purposes. Hear His voice. Feel His hand. Be sensitive to His checks. Even if you question this position on God's guidance, you are living proof of His guidance. How else can you explain the course of your life to this point? "Since my youth, O God, you have taught me, and to this day I declare your marvelous deeds" (Ps. 71:17). You have actually lived your life until now in the manner that has been described.

One time my family climbed the Red Rocks outside Flagstaff, Arizona, to check out Native American dwellings and carvings of a thousand years ago. A nearly vertical climb with no discernible path up the mountain, we had to closely follow Mr. Ballard, who had been there before. Mr. Ballard kept convincing us that it was worth the effort. He would stop every now and then to point to the cave holes. We persevered through ledges that were half steps, clinging to other seeming possibilities, and walked through a couple of dark corridors. The kids were filled with a sense of adventure while as parents we were afraid for them and us. I heard our daughter say, "If you follow Mr. Ballard, you won't fall!" She reminded me of even more important sentiments: "For this God is our God for ever and ever; he will be our guide even to the end (i.e., death)" (Ps. 48:14). As a friend observed, "Why do you need a road map, when you have a guide?"[3]

In addition to personal, family, and work segments of your life, it is now our responsibility to find God's purpose for our *ministry* life. God's vision compels our purposeful involvement. We don't want to fire a shot and then draw the target. On the other hand, we don't want to keep aiming but never shooting. We must find a personal purpose for life within God's eternal vision for the world. I include ministry life with personal vision and purpose, making all of life participate in that unique role that God calls for each of us to carry out and fulfill in the ongoing administration of His kingdom plans.

PERSONAL PARTICIPATION
IN GOD'S PURPOSE

I recall being welcomed into the men's restroom at the lower level of the Washington, D.C., Hilton by the doorman, "Welcome to the place where every man knows what he is about today!" In our deliberation of God's global vision, we do not refer to small purposes that we are about. We are looking at the highest, ultimate purpose of all humanity—to come to love, honor, and serve God—and how we can personally participate in God's ultimate purpose for all humanity—eternal rescue. What God is about!

Personal participation in God's purpose is primarily an outworking of God's ultimate purpose, His kingdom vision. The Old Testament story shows this redemptive plan in action, by providence and special intervention. The epitaph of the Holy Spirit on David's life shows how God's purpose was woven into his life. Nestled in a prophecy about the Messiah, Acts 13:36 reads, "David, after he fulfilled the purpose of God in his own generation, fell asleep."[4] Notice he did not fulfill the purpose of God for a previous or future generation. David knew what he was about for his day and for his own generation.

Notice also that David did not fulfill his own purposes. He greatly wanted to build a great temple to honor God but shelved his own plans under God's guidance. We want to be very careful in the process of discovering the future, that is, God's future. We could be overcome with ungodly ambition, selfish agendas, and wrong motives. Babel's builders attempted to fulfill their own purposes (Gen. 11:4). God acknowledges that power of human ambition and activity: "Nothing which they purpose to do will be impossible for them" (Gen. 11:6 NASB). But the one who resists all pride (1 Pet. 5:5) quickly checks personal ambition. Preposterous ("the wisdom of this world is foolishness in God's sight," 1 Cor. 3:19) and presumptuous purposes, such as the barn builder in the parable (Luke 12:18), aren't encouraged in finding God's personal purpose. Running from book to magazine to movie to journal to fortune cookies from the point of "worldly wis-

dom" to discover and define the future actually confuses life
(see Eccl. 1:8; 12:12). "The wisdom of the wise will perish,
the intelligence of the intelligent will vanish" (Isa. 29:14).
Don't come with your own purposes and let them compete
with God's global, doxological, soteriological purpose.
Gamaliel's wise guarantee applies to our presumptuous,
prideful, predictive initiatives: "For if their purpose or activity is of human origin, it will fail" (Acts 5:38). Personal purpose must conform to God's purpose.

That's how Paul aligned his life. In his complete mentor-
ing list to Timothy, he boldly declared, "you know all about
. . . my purpose" (2 Tim. 3:10). We know the purpose he
received to fulfill the divine agenda. He recounts it in Acts
26:16–18 (NASB):

> But get up and stand on your feet; for this purpose I
> have appeared to you, to appoint you a minister and
> a witness not only to the things which you have seen,
> but also to the things in which I will appear to you;
> rescuing you from the Jewish people and from the
> Gentiles, to whom I am sending you, to open their
> eyes so that they may turn from darkness to light and
> from the dominion of Satan to God, that they may
> receive forgiveness of sins and an inheritance among
> those who have been sanctified by faith in Me.

Paul's personal purpose grasped the divine purpose: "We
proclaim him, admonishing and teaching everyone with all
wisdom, so that we may present everyone perfect in Christ.
To this end [or purpose] I labor, struggling with all his energy, which so powerfully works in me" (Col. 1:28–29). That
was the purpose for which he worked extremely hard but not
in his own energy. Elsewhere he declared, "I consider my life

worth nothing to me, if only I may finish the race and complete the task the Lord Jesus has given me—the task of testifying to the gospel of God's grace" (Acts 20:24).

Just as God's blueprint is not passive and static in the discovery process, so your submission to the Lord's will does not leave you in fatalistic paralysis. Not only does the Bible command you to intentionally pursue knowledge and wisdom (cf. the book of Proverbs, see 2:3–5 for instance); your present life can be the living will of God. Too often we think of the will of God as future, when the present is just as much the will of God. When you please God in the present, you are doing the will of God. It is only by His will that you are alive, awake, active, and possibly alert—breathing and kicking—at this very moment. If you see the future as made up of successive "present(s)", then it is possible for you to fulfill the will of God. As you please God (remember the doxological purpose?), you are in the will of God. Do whatever your hand finds to do with all your heart (Col. 3:23), in the name of Christ (Col. 3:17), to the glory of God (1 Cor. 10:31), and you are living the acceptable life (Rom. 12:1–2; James 4:15). So don't go about trying to find the will of God for the future without living for the pleasure of God in the present. If you are not pleasing God today, a result of *passion* with your focus on *mission,* forget about finding God's will for the future.

One's unique purpose, then, is revealed as Scripture's large purpose gets processed through personal history. God's plans are revealed by submission and obedience. As you live in obedience to what you know is true, you receive more light to show you that whatever good you have done was done through God. Jesus says, "whoever lives by the truth comes into the light, so that it may be seen plainly that what he has done has been done through God" (John 3:21), a verse emphasizing salvation living. Surprise yourself looking backward at any time and even at your last breath that as you obeyed, more light was given, and what you did was through God Himself.

Discovering one's sole purpose is broad and comes through Scripture interacting with life. To an extent, we can find it, write it down, and live by it. Finding God's *unique* role for us arises from ongoing spiritual sensitivity to the God who leads specifically as we yield to Him.[5] Asking God for guidance and leadership provides grounds for our confidence in His purpose. If He has written the playbook and has sequenced my life, I might as well ask Him for leadership in my living out His purpose. In any case, His calling and power are the means by which "every good purpose of [ours] and every act prompted by [our] faith" will be fulfilled (2 Thess. 1:11).

Consider a rather straightforward prayer of Paul for the Colossian church. From the day he had heard of them, he did not cease to pray for them, asking God:

> . . . to fill you with the knowledge of his will through all spiritual wisdom and understanding. And we pray this in order that you may live a life worthy of the Lord and may please him in every way: bearing fruit in every good work, growing in the knowledge of God, being strengthened with all power according to his glorious might so that you may have great endurance and patience. (Colossians 1:9–11)

The grammatical connections within these verses set a comprehensive conclusion to this chapter. The source of our knowledge of God's will is God's filling (cross-reference the role of the Holy Spirit in personal filling and revelation). The knowledge of God's will is in spiritual wisdom and understanding (cross-reference the role of the Holy Bible in finding spiritual wisdom and understanding). Further, we find the crucial need to be filled by God's will in wisdom and understanding in yielding two results: living a worthy life and endurance. We cannot by ourselves live a life worthy of the Lord, which is reflected in a pleasurable, fruit-bearing life in every good work, and growing in the knowledge of God.[6] Neither can we be strengthened by His power to patiently endure life unless we are filled by God's will, wisdom, and understanding.

Qutb Minar, a fourteenth-century tower on the outskirts of Delhi, India, was built to warn the Muslim kingdom of rapacious invaders. In an effort to dissuade suicidal tendencies, much of the tower is presently off limits to tourists. A guide once escorted me to the rampart of the first floor. The brilliant architect had placed windows at the right places on what would have otherwise been a dark passageway. Each window lets in only enough light to illuminate the immediate steps around it. Steps emerge in the dark as you keep climbing, illuminated by the next window.

My tower guide was able to get permission for me from the authorities to climb all the way to the top. He said the windows were shut off, but that he had been that way many times before. Also, he could open the windows to let in light as we climbed farther. He assured me that the next time I climbed to the first floor, I wouldn't need him as much, since my confidence in the light from the windows had grown. The light would get me up there since I had been there before. But the farther I went, I needed him to escort me, to open the windows, to let in more light, to encourage me up the hard way, to keep me from falling, to lift me when I fell, to keep on.

Too often in life I want to see my way all the way to the top, but God has designed life like the architect of the Qutb Minar. There's enough light for the need. As I keep climbing, the next steps become evident. The Bible provides light to my path, and the Holy Spirit escorts me up the stairway of life, opening up windows as needed, encouraging me as I fall.

God's ultimate purpose to bring people to Himself forever—which is our destination—is clear. We have to climb the challenging steps of discerning and fulfilling our personal role in that ultimate purpose by means of the Word and the Spirit. God pursues an eternal, global purpose. God prescribes a personal participation in His eternal, global purpose. I recently read that 70 percent of family-owned businesses will be sold (read "lost") in the first generation, with 85 percent sold off in the second generation. And then I watched the premiere of *A Candle in the Dark*—the story of the father of modern missions, William Carey. Two hundred years later his work done in India still goes and grows strong. I had to ask if I wanted to make passing on a family business my vision, or did I want to serve an eternal God in my vocation. When personal purpose yields to God's purpose, it is doing God's will for you.[7]

God carries a resolve toward you. You will not get lost but will stay found because God found you. He will not abandon His children. He will lead His children as you obey, but not before you obey. So don't worry so much about finding God's will. Think more about doing it, because God sustains a resolve to reach the world. Will you resolve to participate in His ultimate resolve?

Renovating Life

checked my suitcase on a Jakarta to Los Angeles flight, with a change of planes in Hong Kong. As you would expect from my using an illustration about airline baggage, mine did not arrive with me. I filed a lost baggage claims report—citing the tag number, flight number, the color, shape, and make of the suitcase. For three long days, they couldn't find it. Finally, after

> *If you can't see very far ahead, go as far as you can see.*
>
> ❧ DAWSON TROTMAN

spending what seemed like an unauthorized NASA planetary probe joining other lost airline baggage to make up the rings around Saturn, the bag arrived.

The explanation of the temporary loss was simple: The handle had come off of the suitcase, the destination tag had been on the handle, thus airline personnel could not find the destination tag and could not send it on the flight with me. Actually, the baggage depot in Hong Kong had identified the suitcase. They knew it was lost. They even knew it belonged to me from the name tag on the side. They simply didn't know where it was to be sent! The name tag revealed the owner's identity. The kind of entity showed its mission—a suitcase, to carry personal effects. But nothing showed its destination.

Often Christians are like that lost suitcase. They know to whom they belong. They have a name tag attached to them—"Christ followers." Perhaps some details are abbreviated or missing on your particular name tag because you wrote them in a hurry at check-in. Maybe you wrote your last name with only the initials of your first name. Or you wrote your full name but not your full address. Perhaps the phone number is clear but not the street details. Like my lost suitcase, many Christians are not heading toward the right destination. Suitcases don't take responsibility for purposelessness, but airlines and Christians can and should.

I would like to challenge you to get all the details written clearly on your life name tag. If you don't already have it filled out correctly, you'd better get your spiritual life in order. Your passion for the Lord Jesus Christ must supersede your passions in life. Your spiritual life is fundamental and basic to your human journey.

We also know the function of a suitcase. Its "mission" is to carry stuff. Your life also should be clear as to its function—in personal, family, and work life. The mission of your life is to make God look good in these areas of your responsibility. Your mission is to live your life, serve your family, and function at work in a God-honoring way. However, like my suitcase, an apparent reason exists for the detached, lost handle: the bag was carrying too much weight. Sometimes that excess can cause problems.

And where is the bag going? Is it going along with the owner to where the owner wants to go? In God's Vision for this world, you know where your Owner wants you to go. Will you go along with Him? Your life needs a handle that can "handle" not only the suitcase but can display your destination as well. When my bag finally arrived, I took it in for repair. Baggage repairers put a new handle on it, reinforcing it with steel screws for maximum strength. I have used the bag since. The handle has stayed on, and the bag hasn't gotten lost.

What destination tag hangs around your life? If you don't know where you are going, who you are and what you do matters little in the total scheme of God's realities. It also doesn't matter which way you take. "If you don't know where you are heading, you are likely to end up somewhere else" is true about airlines offering "mystery flights"—you don't know where you're going until after takeoff. An article I read said, "Somebody showed up in Bermuda shorts and ended up in Milwaukee." He got "points for optimism."[1] Unfortunately, if you don't know where you are going, any destination becomes justifiable. You may not start up at all. You could be stuck.

I am going to make a bold assertion here. Unless your destination for life adjusts to God's destination[2] (His Vision for the world), then any vision for yourself will be just that—a vision for your Self. You will not be connected to or in compliance with an appropriate vision for yourself. You will become like Israel in the Old Testament, assuming God's salvation was for your good alone. Passion without engagement (cf. the fourth and final set of spiritual disciplines in *Soul Passion*) will turn you into a mere mystic. Your personal mission allows you to be aligned to God's expectations of personal, family, and work life. Those are laudable, though the sturdy building (like the misaligned Bombay hotel) will face backward, away from God's intention. God wants you to build a life that is visionary—toward His international Vision, in which every segment of your life is visionary as well—toward His Vision.

Draw two circles on a sheet of paper. Identify one as yours by putting your initials on top of it. In that circle, write out the central vision of your life—your main ambition, your primary pursuit. Be honest with yourself. This exercise is for you alone to see, so don't give the answer you think you *should* give. Just reflect present reality. On top of the other circle, God's circle, write LJC, for the Lord Jesus Christ. Inside this circle, write out His central Vision. (You have some clue about what it is from the previous chapters.) Now comes the hard question: As you conceptually overlay your vision with His Vision, how complementary and compatible are the two? If your circle doesn't coalesce with Jesus' Vision, you are trivializing life, reducing life, and facing the wrong way. In this chapter, we hope to find a way to place your circle, a small one, inside Jesus' circle for an intentional life future.

Like the British architect's assumption in sending his hotel plans to the builder, it is right to have an oceanfront building face the ocean. However, most Christians build a good foundation and an impressive ground floor but face away into a busy city. They accept the Creator's plans for their salvation and their daily lives but not His Vision for the world. They are like strong, beautiful buildings—facing backward.

It is not physically easy to move a huge building, but it can be done. St. Josephat's Basilica in Milwaukee, Wisconsin, was formerly a post office in Chicago. After the great Chicago fire, Polish immigrants with a vision to build a cathedral dismantled the massive post office, salvaged the stone blocks, brought them to Milwaukee, and rebuilt them into a gorgeous basilica. Your life may need to be deconstructed, moved, and rebuilt again into a more glorious vision. Until then, like the rooms of the Bombay Taj, you can rearrange your life so the occupants can at least view the ocean. When you please God in your daily mission, you accomplish the mission of God's glory. To that extent, your room is enjoyable. But you want more than enjoyment. As you grow spiritually, you want to bear fruit for God's ultimate purpose. You want your circle of vision to connect, merge, and submit to Jesus' Vision. Unlike the hotel, you can turn life around to face the ocean, attuned to Jesus' Vision for your life. Or, you can break it down, brick by brick, and build a new one to fulfill God's Vision for you.

How can you "make a difference" or "make your life count" for God's Vision? The deeper biblical counterpart of "making a difference" terminology is "bearing fruit."[3] As a "results" metaphor, it relates to internal fruit—the fruit of the Spirit (Gal. 5) and of righteousness (Phil. 1:11) in character (cf. virtues) and to ministry. Jesus chose us "to go and bear fruit—fruit that will last" (John 15:16). Paul prays that the Colossians will bear fruit in every good work (Col. 1:10). Internal fruit must precede and exceed the ministry. I hope we never forget that we can't make our lives count for God, make a difference, or bear fruit in our own strength. The whole point of Jesus' metaphor of the vine and branches (John 15) was to insist that we couldn't make our lives count without an integral, spiritual connection with Him, the one true Vine. "I am the vine; you are the branches. If a man remains in me and I in him, he will bear much fruit; apart from me you can do a few things" (John 15:5). You may have gotten lazy in your reading and missed that last part . . . the last part of Jesus' words actually says, "apart from me you can do NOTHING!"[4]

Allow me to reiterate the *primacy of passion for Jesus Christ* before we go on to ministry vision. My suspicion about hard-driving, vision-bent, "can-do" Christian leaders is that we make our ministries our passion. Jesus wants us to begin and stay in an acknowledgment of inability, indigence, and impoverishment that is only correctable by a lifeline connection to Him. He desires for us to eradicate self-sufficiency, even if we have already gone past self-centeredness. The moment we think we are indispensable to Him and that we can accomplish something for God, we have abandoned the vital source for any ministry accomplishment. We need to be attached to Him whether we can discern how we ought to bear fruit or not.

Further, our passion for Jesus Christ must even exceed our passion for His passion. We must distinguish between our affection for our Leader and a commitment to His cause. We dare not mistake our dedication to His cause as love for Him. A person is always more than his cause—he has to be, if his cause is to be justifiable. When we understand this, we will stick to a cause even if the results aren't what we expect them to be.[5] Chambers alerts us: "Beware of any work for God that causes or allows you to avoid concentrating on Him. A great number of Christian workers worship their work. The only concern of Christian workers should be their concentration on God."[6]

Spiritual purposes—underlying passion—precede His ministry purposes, His ultimate Vision for me. God turns profit out of unprofitable servants and when He looks for fruit, He will not be disappointed (Luke 13:6) because we stayed connected to Him. Our fruit becomes His fruit. He remains the passion *of* life, with commitment to ministry becoming a passion *in* life.

RENOVATING THE HOUSE: PROCESSING LIFE UNDER GOD'S VISION

To make a difference for God's global purpose, to not disappoint ourselves during the final "house" inspection, you will need to renovate the inside of the building of your life. Take advantage of the majestic ocean view. The scenery doesn't need to be lost just because you've messed up on position, orientation, and direction in the past. It is best to have the whole building facing aright, but in a fallen world, we sometimes must put up with a less than perfect orientation—for the short term or the long term. Eventually, if we don't renovate the rooms to view the ocean, we are missing out on the purpose of the location. We can renovate the house (the sectors of our life) to partial fulfillment of God's Vision for the world. As believers, we already have a live-in Master General Contractor. This new interior will focus vision to identify our distinct Christian identity and mission so that faulty, fuzzy visions don't claim the multidimensional missions in life.

How would you, for example, go about renovating your life under God's Vision for the world? You might start by rearranging, removing, or restoring the "furniture" inside. This is the least active of all responses to God's ultimate Vision. For example, you provide hospitality to a missionary visiting your city. Though inconvenient, you loan him or her a car that you can probably live without for a week. You give money to world evangelism through your church. As opportunities are presented to you, you decide on a case-by-case basis to participate financially in parachurch projects. You are reactive in this stance, but that is still better than being self-oriented in your pursuits. However, if any of your other segments of life demand immediate or intensified attention, God's ultimate Vision goes out the window in this scenario.

Most Christians fall into the practice of rearranging the furniture to enjoy the greatest benefits with the least expense. I wouldn't call them purposeful and intentional in life. They are good, solid, reliable people—the kind you want to see as citizens of your country, neighbors, and employees. In this condition, however, they are not likely to be available much to God's Vision.

Extensive renovation of a house is no small thing, however. It can actually cost you a bit—and it can hurt. You have to think differently about your insides. Should you turn the formal dining room into a bedroom? Or your extra living space into an area comfortable for sharing hospitality? What about the floors? What kind of carpet do you want? How do the counters match the new floor? And the cupboards—should you replace, repair, or repaint them? New furniture? What kind do you want? How do the new pieces coordinate with the rest of the house and its new orientation? Renovation takes time, money, energy, and commitment. Expect your house to look disheveled for some time as you rearrange the interior.

Taking this analogy further, how do you undertake an extensive renovation of *life*? You actually take the segments of life and set objectives for them in keeping with God's international Vision. You move from a passive or reactive awareness to active appropriation of His Vision in your life. You process each segment and subsegment of your life under God's Vision to bring people to Himself. You submit every area of life for possible dismantling, all the way down to the foundation if necessary, in order to restore or rebuild that part of the structure in keeping with God's ultimate Vision.

Remember the "What?" "So what?" and "Now what?" sequence of exploration that we have applied to so many areas of our discussion in Book One and Book Two? This includes the questions: *What does God say? So what does it mean to my life? and Now what do I do?*

I want you to:

> ask those three questions,

> analyze your answers, and

> apply strategies toward God's ultimate purpose for your life—His Vision for the world.

The "What?" question is "What is God's Vision?"—*gaining the worship of people worldwide by bringing them to Himself*. Now apply the "So what?" and "Now what?" questions to each dimension of your life. For a start, let me suggest some ways to orient the dimensions of your life to the Vision in renovating the room and spaces in your life structure.

PERSONAL LIFE: SPIRITUAL

So What?

Become more sensitive to God's concerns for humanity.

Now What?

Are you willing to sacrifice and even suffer for the sake of His Vision? How might you reorder your spiritual life in order to fulfill God's Vision? How can you study the Bible, not only for personal refreshment but also to understand and obey the dimensions of God's concern for all people?

Consult the "TARGET" of Goals (in Book Two, *Soul Mission*, [page 124–131]) and the planning worksheet to write and implement objectives and action steps. Tomorrow morning, make a list of your possessions that you think you can't live without—a house, a car, a boat, a talent—whatever possesses you. Are you willing to use or sacrifice them for the Vision? Don't be afraid of being honest with yourself. God understands your fear and hesitation. As long as you have them, you ought to enjoy them. Just don't move from enjoying them to loving them. If you can't give them to God, at least give Him permission to take them back.

PERSONAL LIFE: INTELLECTUAL

So What?

Become aware of how God's salvation sweeps across the globe to bring people to Himself.

Now What?

Send a gift of twenty-five dollars to six mission agencies to get on their mailing lists. Then read their magazines for awareness and possible involvement. In the next three months, make sure your next book to read will be a world-missions-oriented book.

PERSONAL LIFE: PHYSICAL

So What?

Consider an overseas exposure trip for a change of perspective on how you live and spend your money.

Seek out acquaintances with new immigrants and international students to inquire how life here compares with life in their homelands.

Now What?

Within a month, look for an opportunity to volunteer time in a lower-income neighborhood. In the same month, do an Internet search of organizations that facilitate short-term mission trips overseas.

PERSONAL LIFE: FINANCIAL

So What?

Share what you have with those who have nothing.

Now What?

Are you expecting a windfall (such as I am with the publication of this series—high hopes!) from stock market surprises or gains in investments? What percentage of any new income will go into unleashing money toward God's Vision? Your stewardship of finances must include giving to the cause of God's global Vision. Increase your giving to ministry and missions by 1 percent every year. In six months, start putting away an additional amount each month to finance an overseas trip. I know a man who lives on 5 percent of his income and funds large projects for the Vision.

PERSONAL LIFE: MATERIAL

So What?

Use your house to entertain guests from other countries.

Now What?

How can you share hospitality, food, and clothing with those who are less fortunate than you? You might invite international students along with their families to your home during the holiday season. I like to take overseas-ministry guests to a clothing store near our home to get them something they could not afford to buy.

Or, I try not to keep more than a dozen ties in my closet. Neckties have a sneaky way of entering your wardrobe during birthdays and gift-giving holidays with permanent staying power for years! Now that business casual has become the norm in North Dallas, we even started "A Tie to *RREACH*" program to alleviate this common "tie" problem. We solicit ties from men to send to pastors overseas. Even though neckties are not of much practical help, they identify the Christian pastor in many African countries! A Sunday school class in a large church volunteered to have all the men bring in ties for a month. One man brought in thirty ties. We had boxes and boxes of ties. (Some of them should have been retired decades ago for displays at fashion museums.) My office took half a day to sort them out and threw out the bad ones. We now have a policy that "only ties that a person would presently wear and wouldn't feel embarrassed giving away directly" should be given.

What about emptying your wardrobe to contribute to organizations that take in used clothing in good condition to pass along to students and other needy people?

PERSONAL LIFE: RECREATIONAL

So What?

Free up some time to volunteer services at church or a nonprofit agency.

Now What?

Next Sunday ask around (church leaders, the evangelism or missions committees) for volunteer opportunities in your town. Choose two opportunities that meet needs that you are sensitive to and offer your services to them on a weekly or monthly basis. God will work out the hours and tasks in the right combination for you and them—after they recover from the shock of your offer of time.

PERSONAL LIFE: SOCIAL

So What?

Move from your comfort zone into a cross-cultural relationship.

Challenge the inner circle of your friends to prioritize God's global Vision.

Now What?

Befriend an international student at a local university this semester, assisting with personal needs, and enjoying some time with that person three times in the next six months. It won't be long before that person hears about what God is doing around the world. That's true in my case. These people often end up in my inner circle—they would not be there if this were not the case. I have hundreds of acquaintances, but my inner circle of friends knows that my priority is God's global Vision—and they still accept me into their lives. Some of them even left careers or retired early to join me full-time in the fulfillment of the Great Vision.

FAMILY LIFE: SPOUSE AND KIDS

So What?

Encourage your family to think outside the boundaries of familiar color, race, class, and language.

Take your family on an overseas trip.

Now What?

Extend friendship to someone outside your zone of familiarity. Invite a "foreign" family to a meal and overnight stay during the next holiday break.

Perhaps the finest investment of our resources as a family has been in planning and investing in a service trip overseas each year. We are exposed to cultures, environments, and needs that make us more generous and open-minded. We've been in danger, in laughter, in embarrassment, in tears, but all in family ministry. This is my small attempt in bringing His Vision to the level of my mission toward raising my family rightly.

FAMILY LIFE: EXTENDED

So What?

Involve your extended family (siblings, parents, grand-kids) in God's Vision.

Now What?

Our situation is rather unique in that most of our extended family is into the Vision. My only encouragement would be to get their eyes off "material" things and learn to become better givers to the Vision. This year, pass on two specific opportunities to each of your siblings, allowing them to consider God's Vision in their giving or service, according to ability.

WORK LIFE

Let's face it. Your occupation, whether at home, school, business, or profession, "occupies" you. Except "occupation" becomes "pre"-occupation for many of us. We get so busy that there is no energy left for the previous two dimensions of life. Here, the "So what?" and the "Now what?" questions can yield extensive plans, but their value, relative to the central responsibilities in life, must be kept in mind.

A friend of mine spends more than two hundred nights away from home each year traveling for his company. Many things in his life are out of balance. When I visit his home office, it is filled with unattended papers and unanswered correspondence—years old. He travels so much that he smells like an airplane. He constantly eats on the run at fast-food restaurants. You often can find him tied to his cell phone, rearranging meetings and flight schedules. He possesses one of the finest business minds I know with an aptitude for facts and figures like I will never acquire—reading financial statements does not occur on my wish list, let alone my want or work list! He sees his work as his "calling." (I have added a brief section on "calling" immediately following this outline.)

So What?

Use your vocation as the place and platform to introduce people to salvation or service.

Ken wrote me a note about how his career has turned into a calling:

> The Lord led me to the book of Hebrews and the first five chapters convinced me that even Jesus needed a calling on His life. Somehow I felt that I needed a calling and I was going to let Him call me to anything. One evening I was reading Paul's writings and he mentioned "Zenas the lawyer." A Christian lawyer seemed somewhat of an oxymoron but it was a seed the Lord used to get me into a new direction. I have just completed thirteen years as an attorney here! My partner is a Christian and this last year we have seen around forty people come to faith in our office.

David and his son have graciously mowed our lawn for the last ten years. Each time I see them mowing or trimming the grass, I am overwhelmed with their generosity. It is far easier to give money than service to people, but these guys are true servants. They have not only extended their work life to serve us; they find many natural opportunities to spread the gospel among non-Christians because of the quality and consistency of their work. They have turned lawn mowing from a vocation into a calling.

Now What?

Find one person to share Christ with during this calendar year. Start a regular Bible study with a few Christians in your workplace.

Ravi works for a large communications company in his city. When he got found by Jesus a couple of years ago, he started viewing his vocation as the arena to fulfill God's vision for the world. In just two years, he has initiated eight weekly Bible studies that meet before office hours. That's bringing the Vision of God to bear on life missions. That accomplishes God's glory in bringing people to Himself.

Charlie, a postman, serves a hundred nationalities of people on his route. Taking personal responsibility for their lack of awareness of his Lord Jesus, he wondered how he could turn his career into a calling, an opportunity to serve God. He mastered information about his customers—their native countries and mother languages—then ordered the New Testament in their languages. Since giving the books to them would conflict with company policy, he hit upon a terrific idea. Mail them to his constituency! Naturally he knew their addresses, paid the postage, mailed them, and because he knows his route, hand delivered them to the ones whose addresses he placed on the packets. Why shouldn't they receive Bibles mailed by someone who knows them, when they receive junk from anonymous senders? He has already shared the Bible with the Arabic-speaking community. He now targets another language group.

That's bringing the Vision of God to bear on the segmented (personal, family, work) missions in life. That postman accomplishes God's glory by introducing God's Word to the ones who have never heard the Good News of Jesus.

CALLING

Many fine people hold the view that a "calling" concerns their businesses and professions. They sense a "calling" individually to their work.[7] Since this view of a calling calls for excellence and hard work, I resist the temptation to critique it too harshly. I know what it means, but it is not sustainable biblically.[8]

The sustained emphasis on "calling" in Scripture pertains to God's calls to salvation (cf. Rom. 8:28; 11:29; 1 Cor. 1:26) and its implications (e.g., holiness, 1 Thess. 4:7; 2 Tim. 1:9); to hope (Eph. 1:18), including suffering for doing good (1 Pet. 2:20; possibly also Rev. 17:14); and to glory (Phil. 3:14; 1 Pet. 5:10). In salvation, we distinguish between "the general call" of God that goes out to everybody, and the "efficacious call" toward those who would believe.[9] The "elect" are diligent to make their calling and election (to salvation) sure (2 Pet. 1:10).

In Scripture, we also find that "calling," "choosing," and "ordaining" relate only to ministry—the fulfillment of God's Vision for the world. Whether it is Abraham (Gen. 12:1), Moses (Exod. 3:2–10), Joshua (Num. 27:18–23; Josh. 1:1–9), Deborah (Judg. 4–5), Gideon (Judg. 6:11–14); Nehemiah (Neh. 1), Isaiah (Isa. 6:1–8), Jeremiah (Jer. 1:5), Ezekiel (Ezek. 1:9), Amos (Amos 7:14–15), Mary (Luke 1:26ff.), the Lord Jesus (Heb. 5:4–6), the disciples (Mark 1:16–20; 2:13–17), or Paul (Acts 16:9–10), each was "assigned to each his task" by God Himself (1 Cor. 3:5). The work assignments of biblical characters fulfilled God's march throughout history. So let's not call any job or profession "a calling." However, these work assignments—our work at hand, our mission to our obligations—could fulfill the Vision. When we fulfill the Vision in our jobs, it is then that our jobs become "callings."[10]

Our calling is to the Vision. Our excellence in our vocations is simply a mission that must be processed within and toward that Vision. We can turn our job description and our work obligations into a calling as we fulfill God's Vision to bring the world to Himself. If we don't turn work into a calling, we are using it as a means to income, sustenance, and profit. We still must excel at it. We still must apply biblical principles and character to it. We still must do our work heartily as to the Lord, to God's glory. We can pursue our mission to glorify God in our job, but our calling is to a larger Vision than work excellence and business success.

Remember my two hundred-nights-away-from-home friend who considered his career a calling? My question to my busy brother would be: How does his mission to glorify God in his job accomplish the Vision of God to bring people to Himself? He could do this in two ways: (1) by becoming a *witnessing influence* for God's Vision in his job—to become the instrument of God's salvation calling of those around him. But not during work hours! Or (2) by becoming a *mobilizer* for the Vision on his job—but not during work hours either. Each person he comes across is a candidate for either salvation or for participation in the Vision. If he goes about intentionally witnessing for Christ by example, prayer, and word, God will bring people to Himself. If he mobilizes people for Christ—by challenging Christian colleagues to embrace God's Vision for the world, he has turned his daily work into a purposeful role for the kingdom. If he works to earn money to give to God's Vision, he takes his ongoing mission and converts it into a "calling." If he uses his business expertise to serve on the board of a Christian nonprofit organization that implements the Vision, he has invested his talents to serve the Vision. He is mobilizing people and money for Christ's priority in the world.

His job in itself won't be God's call. His job would be

God's placement—he is placed there by God to fulfill His Vision. God has designed him in a way that brings him satisfaction and income out of his work. But his work assignment is not his *Christian* calling. His work is the place, the platform, the pulpit, where God's Vision for the world can be carried out. I would ask if he were seizing the opportunities to introduce God's salvation in the circle of his influence. Is he mobilizing people and resources for the Vision? To the extent that he is not, he fails in it as a Christian calling. As part of his job, if he includes God's Vision into his personal objectives at work, he is fulfilling his Christian calling. His income-producing vocation—used until now to support his family obligations in direct command of Scripture—changes into a biblical calling as he uses his placement to witness or recruit for the kingdom and to evangelize or mobilize in obedience to the direct commands of Scripture. God's calling and faith-prompted action toward personal purpose are connected again in Paul's prayer, "that our God may count you worthy of his calling, and that by his power he may fulfill every good purpose of yours and every act prompted by your faith" (2 Thess. 1:11). It takes active, action-oriented faith to turn vocation into a biblical calling in personal purpose.

God designs us for our work assignments, opens up ways to find those appropriate assignments, and expects our faithfulness to Him in those places. "Slaves" ought to be pleasers of God (Eph. 6:5–7). Yet, in those places of work, He calls us to join His Vision. Before you find out God's Vision for you, find out about God's Vision and see how you can get your life facing that direction.

Kudos to you in renovating your life, processing every aspect of everyday life under His Vision. I close this important section with a longer citation from Oswald Chambers—

the paragraph from which his powerful devotional book was titled:

> If we lose "the heavenly vision" God has given us, we alone are responsible—not God. We lose the vision because of our own lack of spiritual growth. If we do not apply our beliefs about God to the issues of everyday life, the vision God has given us will never be fulfilled. The only way to be obedient to "the heavenly vision" is to give our utmost for His highest—our best for His glory. This can be accomplished only when we make a determination to continually remember God's vision. But the acid test is obedience to the vision in the details of our everyday life—sixty seconds out of every minute, and sixty minutes out of every hour, not just during times of personal prayer or public meetings. . . . We cannot bring the vision to fulfillment through our own efforts, but must live under its inspiration until it fulfills itself.[11]

How can we bring the Vision to fulfillment by offering our efforts while living under its inspiration for its fulfillment? That takes turning the building around! From renovating the interior, let's turn next to reorienting the entire structure.

Reorienting Life—
Focusing Personal
Vision

Realizing that he was lost, the hot air balloonist reduced height and yelled to a man in an open field below: "Excuse me, can you tell me where I am?"

The man below shouted back: "You are in a hot air balloon, hovering thirty feet above this field."

"You must work in engineering," said the balloonist.

"I do," replied the man. "How did you know?"

"Well," said the bal-loonist, "everything you have told me is technically correct, but it's of no use to anyone."

> *No noise is so emphatic as one you are trying not to listen to.*
>
> ❧ C. S. LEWIS

The man below said, "You must work in the planning department!"

"I do," replied the balloonist, "but how did you know?"

"Well," said the man, "you don't know where you've come from, where you are, nor where you're going, but you expect me to be able to help. You're in the same position you were before we met, but now it's my fault!"

In discussing the Intentional Life, we have talked about (1) our unifying *passion*—loving the person of God Himself,

(2) our unifying *mission*—promoting the program of God's glory, and (3) our unifying *vision*—serving the plans for God's international kingdom. As with passion and mission, there is a personal dimension to the vision of God. Our personal vision *in* life intentionalizes life. You and I can be technically correct but practically useless. We are to begin by knowing where we have been in life, where we are in life, and where we are going in life in order to receive help.

I tell graduate theology students that we need to devote time to three large subjects. We must exegete Scripture, culture, and our lives. May I help you begin to exegete your life as seriously as you should study God's Word and His world?

Why study your life? Because there is only one you and no one else can study it for you. That's what it takes to live intentionally. We are not dialoguing here about simply remodeling the building or merely rearranging the furniture of your life. We are talking about tearing it down and rebuilding it, about reorienting the building to the Architect's expectation. It's turning the building around so that your superstructure faces the ocean. I don't want you facing the wrong way or running the wrong way with all that the Lord has endowed you in the past, granted you in the present, and prepared for you in the future.

Writing this section is not easy for me because it carries far-reaching implications for every reader. I enter these pages as a sacred responsibility. But I must write them because too many Christians are oriented wrongly. They live reliable lives as good Christians and they think they are headed right, but they are facing the wrong direction. Most of their missions are in good process, but their future visions are disoriented and discontinuous with their ultimate purpose on earth and disconnected from God's ultimate purpose for the earth.

They are like Douglas Corrigan who, in 1938, departed New York City on a solo flight bound for Los Angeles. Twenty-eight hours and three thousand miles later, he landed in Dublin, Ireland. Why? He knew how to fly solo, but he didn't know how to read the compass. He followed the wrong end of his compass needle. He became known as "Wrong Way" Corrigan. You should not continue the legend. Keep the plane of your life flying, but don't read the wrong end of the compass. Be sure you know both the specific destination (God's Vision) and the general direction, even if you don't know the details of your route.

It is also hard to write this section because too many believers start out with the right destination in mind but get seduced when they become successful. They default from the right direction when they reach the latter part of their lives. It could happen to me if it happened to King Saul. Gifted and talented, Saul, who was a cut above the rest, the man chosen by God to rule His people, lost direction and destination in life. His spiritual passion became diffused. He lost his heart for God. His personal mission became confused; he became obsessed with killing David rather than with fulfilling the obligations of his monarchy. His personal vision was focused on extending his sovereignty into the unforeseen future. Eventually, he fell on his sword to take his own life.

That misdirection happened to Solomon as well. What a great beginning he had! Offered all the blessings of life, he asked for wisdom and discernment. Yet his passion became divided, his mission attended his divided passions, and his vision for YHWH's theocratic, global kingship atrophied. Earlier in this book you read King Solomon's powerful temple dedicatory prayer for the nations. He finally succumbed to selfish agendas, however. His personal vision did not concede to the divine vision, even though he knew it well.

David, caught between Saul and Solomon, provides an excellent portrait of a life that must be continuously reoriented, even when disorientation sets in. While life is like a building, it is not fully like a physical building. Yes, we can do some renovating on the inside, rearranging walls and furniture, but turning a building around—reorienting it—is extremely difficult. Likewise, reorienting one's life is not easy, but it is necessary and possible. The spiritual life process is basically a series of defaults and restarts, disorientation followed by reorientation, sin followed by repentance. Long periods of time in the same spiritual direction toward the destination distinguish the mature Christian from the immature one.

The impossibility of a perfect focus should not keep us from hitting the refresh button of our lives once in a while. When we know our focus, we know what we must return to, what reorientation takes. It is a sad state of affairs if we don't know God's Vision at all, for then we just live randomly. The Intentional Life doesn't protect us from sin, but it does keep us from sleepwalking through life. It also keeps us from being seduced by a myriad of needs around us, left to hopeless tears, or encrusted in isolation.

As you would expect, reorienting life is no small undertaking. For some it may not be a turnaround so much as building a new wing (which the Bombay Taj hotel did). For others, parts of the building may have to be torn down and rebuilt in the same place—like many an upper-class home. Yet others, like St. Josephat's Basilica, will tear down a building, move the material, and reconstruct a new vision.[1] Pursuing a personal vision calls for a radical alteration of lifestyle. This is made possible only by yielding to the preeminence of the lordship of Christ in successive, decisive acts.

How do we go about reorienting life—discovering and implementing personal vision in life as a subset of God's Vision? Your personal vision will be your ministry life, your life of service.

To keep the parallel columns, let me finish the diagram clarifying passion, mission, and vision "of" life and passion, mission, and vision "in" life, which I introduced in Book Two, *Soul Mission*.

"Of" God-Oriented	Passion "of" Life	Mission "of" Life	Vision "of" Life
Identity and nature/ shared with spiritual Christians	Person of God— loving Him	Glory of God— honoring Him	Work of God— serving Him
"In" World-related	Passions "in" Life	Missions "in" Life	Visions "in" Life
Function and impact/ shared with non and carnal and spiritual Christians	Other loves	Daily responsibilities	Future service

Discovering your unique purpose—your personal, future vision—within the large Vision of God requires a serious look at your past and present as sources of a life being unfolded for prospective service. God has not only prepared good works from eternity for you to fulfill (Eph. 2:10) but has been preparing you all of your life for today as well as tomorrow. Let me suggest several tools over the next three chapters that you may use for finding direction in this critical matter of discerning personal vision for your immediate future. I recommend that you read, process, and apply these tools prayerfully and carefully.

PROCESSING YOUR PAST—
THE STAR-SCAR SKETCH

When you are lost in the woods, a local hunter can guide you out of the forest because he has access to information from the very trees that seem to daunt you. Those who explored the forest before you got there actually marked out certain trees for direction, aptly called "marker trees." You can get anywhere as long as you locate just one marker tree, for each carries a guidance pattern.

Similarly, the Star-Scar Sketch helps you to discover marker trees and discern patterns that can lead you out of the woods of your mundane existence. Your life will not be daunting as you study what God has been doing in creating, shaping, and leading your life in the past for the future. He has been preparing you for what He has prepared for you to do (Eph. 2:10).

Since you are a unique person at a particular time in human history, you need to understand the biography of God in the dimensions of your life up until now. Your autobiographical remembrance of past facts, events, experiences, and interpretations of them will provide insight and resources for understanding and embarking on your future. Some memories will stick out more than others. Some are more painful than the rest and would seem best to be forgotten. A Christian view of the past, however, affirms God's superintendence in our lives in spite of its silliness, stupidity, and sins. The Lord has been watching over our lives the entire way. God excels in working all things for our good and for His glory. We do not want to fall into Israel's unwillingness to interpret history with God's hand in mind. They did not have hearts to know or minds to understand, eyes to see or ears to hear (Deut. 29:4). Even when we did not acknowledge Him during stubborn moments of rebellion, our lives were not outside His control. We will experience the consequences of the past, but He specializes in salvage, repair, and reusability. We are products of our past, but not prisoners of it.

WHAT'S IN YOUR "STARS"?

To study your past and understand your history, I would like you to construct a Star-Scar Sketch.[2] I suggest that you add this exercise into your designated time with God—away from noise and activity. Have your Bible, notebook, and a pen to fill in a *"star map" like the one on the next page.* Remember as much you can.[3] Write as much you want. You will actually be filling out this sketch for the rest of your life.

1. Draw a straight line representing your lifetime from birth to the present.

2. Divide the line into convenient period segments starting from birth to your present age. You could do it in five- or ten-year periods.

Or divide the line by less distinct periods. Each life is unique and you may find other chronological markers that are more convenient for your personal understanding.

3. Above this line, I want you to write out your "stars." These stars are not astrological interpretations of astronomical phenomena. Rather, they stand for the highlights, significant events, and memories you love to live by. When you think about them, you wish you could go through them again. These are the true, good, and beautiful events or periods in your life—incidents that produced joy when they happened and still do now in your memory.

These can be anything that brings you sheer delight in remembering, such as:

> getting your first bicycle

➢ an early romantic relationship

➢ changing schools, jobs, cities, etc.

➢ coming to embrace the Lord Jesus Christ as your personal Savior

➢ making the team or an extraordinary sports performance

➢ getting married, having children

➢ evangelistic results

➢ special spiritual days—baptism, confirmation, ordination

➢ promotions and/or accolades

➢ retirement

➢ seeing your children succeed, and so on.

Your star map might look like this diagram:

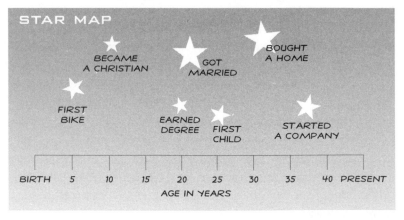

The particular selection of these stars discloses many important factors about you. They reveal some of your motivations. They tell you if you are driven by your possessions, relationships, appearance, etc. Since we human beings are units, constitutionally "whole" and "complex," we are energized by more than one motive. So look for motivational patterns in your listings. If getting your first bicycle, first car, or first house are listed, then you could be alerted in your memory to dominant drives and personal stimuli.

Why do you want to "study your stars"? What you list as highlights communicates your *drives*. Your drives relate to your passions *in* life. If winning a non-Christian to Jesus was a "star," you will be emotionally charged with evangelistic impetus. If buying your first car is listed there, external possessions are important to you. Your passions in life often follow these drives.

Stars also show your *defects*. A thin line divides legitimate "motivations" from spiritual "temptations" that could turn into transgression. If accolades and recognition consistently occur as stars on the lifeline, you will need to beware of several temptations. For example, some people enjoy goal-oriented tasks. They may be driven by the need for approval, or they may control their environment for the sake of self-honor. Such people may even acquire "trophy" spouses and children; they may have huge egos that get in the way of loving relationships. If graduating from high school, college, or a particular institution gave you your identity, watch out for the arrogance of knowledge. Passions in life *attempt* to take over what should be the one true passion of your life.

You may also discern spiritual *desires* in your stars list. Look at your list to see where you were enraptured in spiritual joys. A friend consistently talks about the intense period of joy and "walking in the Spirit" that he experienced in his late twenties. He claims he has not experienced the same spiritual intensity in thirty years. These spiritual highs form a part of his star memories. I asked him what accounted for times of such spiritual depth and passion. He lists the following—Scripture memory, abandonment to God's future, spiritual involvement with nonbelievers, and a church. I went back to Revelation 2 as a model, where the Lord Jesus chastised the Ephesian church for leaving their first love. Jesus challenged them to remember the deeds they were involved in first, and to do them in repenting and returning to their first love.

I asked my friend if he is involved in Scripture memory today. "No!" he replied. I asked further, "Have you placed your future in God's hands?" While he didn't answer immediately, the answer to that question was evident in his lifestyle. He is now extremely wealthy, spent nearly a million dollars in tearing down and building a new home, and is pretty much responsible for generating extraordinary income by putting business deals together. His future doesn't appear to depend on God too much. At least his lifestyle doesn't reveal that it does.

"How many non-Christians have heard the gospel from you?" I asked.

"None, maybe one," he answered.

"Are you involved with a church?"

"No. I have just bought a place by a lake and spend weekends there."

Well, that explains a part of his problem. Unless he identifies the desires, decides on objectives, and acts upon those desires and decisions, he will not come close to the intensity he experienced in his younger days. He has left, not simply lost, his first love—the best and only resource for discerning personal vision.

There may be some ministry *direction* in your stars. If a

pattern of stars relates to ministries in the past, you may view them as key confirmations of the kind of ministry that may capture your life in the future. Find out if a particular pattern of stars stopped at any time and think about why you find a gap or halt to them. Did the stars begin again? Why was there a reason for the gap? Why and when did they restart? Are you still experiencing these stars at present?

Your stars list reveals your drives, defects, desires, and some direction. Take these into account as you seek to understand your vision under God's salvation Vision. I am often asked if one should write out the stars as they were experienced in the past or as they are viewed now. You need to work from your current perspective. For example, one young man said his stars are made up of sleeping with women to fulfill his sexual appetite—at the time, that had been a "positive" for him, but that's not what will be helpful. I am assuming some sense of godliness as you do this exercise. This chart is not meant for non-Christians or for those knowingly living in sin. Not a single person that I know who lived in carnality in the past has viewed past license as star times upon present interpretation. I suggest that you write the event as you experienced it then, but *interpret* it now by way of God's perspective. You'll be amazed how much you have grown spiritually.

WHAT ABOUT YOUR "SCARS"?

More important for discovering personal vision and ministry than the stars of your life are the memories of your "scars." Now for the next step.

4. Below the sketch line of your life, write out your "scars." Scars provide a metaphor for life too. There is no completely safe life. Every person who can remember can

recall scars. Here I want you to discern scars that are still so fresh in your mind that you can relive them if you give them the power to return. Your insides flood with pain—sadness, bitterness, horror, anger, and disappointment. These convey the low points of your life. You would rather not remember them, but they have lodged themselves firmly in your memory, appearing at uncanny moments as ghosts from the past. Perhaps you are going through such a low point right now.

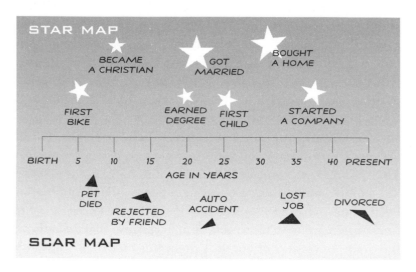

Since God runs a no-waste economy, we can be confident that suffering is not arbitrary in God's schematic. There is no such word as "accident," "mistake," or "slow" in God's vocabulary. In your serious sufferings, your passion for God allows you to give Him the benefit of the doubt, trusting that He had a reason for the troubles you've seen.

God also runs a multitrack economy. He accomplishes several critical matters through your affliction. In your suffering, God not only proves His loving Fatherhood (Prov.

3:11–12; Heb. 12:7ff.; Rev. 3:19); He also refines your faith (1 Pet. 1:6–7), contains your conceit (2 Cor. 12:7), displays His grace and strength (2 Cor. 12:9–10), and develops perseverance (James 5:11) so that you may share in His holiness (Heb. 12:10). "Later on, however, [God's discipline] produces a harvest of righteousness and peace for those who have been trained by it" (Heb. 12:11).[4]

SCARS TO MINISTRY TO MISSION

In terms of personal vision, a part of spiritual maturity comes from suffering. You will not only know and be right, but you will also *do* right as a result of being trained rightly by suffering. Because God specializes in optimizing every situation of your life, He is able to turn weaknesses into strength and work all things together for good. I suggest that your suffering indicates arenas for future service. Part of the training of suffering is to develop commitment, character, and calling in the context of a brief life. In this way, you can comfort others with the same comfort that you have received from God, who is the source of all comfort (2 Cor. 1:2–7).

Buck Pottery, near Gruene, Texas (nine miles south of nowhere), holds process patents for their "handcrafted, wood-fired stoneware." Quality craftsmen, in time-honored tradition and guarded technique, produce beautiful and useful stoneware. The clay is thrown on a potter's wheel, then glazed and fired in a wood-burning kiln to twenty-four hundred degrees Fahrenheit. The wood firing creates a unique natural glaze, the result of wood ash melting on the pottery. Terry Buck explained the technical process:

> Sand off the rough edges with a scrubbing pad, dry, decorate, and glaze them, and then fire them. As it vitrifies and matures, it completely hardens at its

strongest point, at the upper range of temperature, twenty-four hundred degrees in a kiln. As the fire with the wood melts the ash, the pottery actually carries the markings of the fire!

The scars you remember are the "markings of the fire," not only to make you more beautiful but stronger and more useful as well. Fire-marked scars give some direction as to how God wants you to fulfill the Vision. "If you will receive yourself in the fires of sorrow, God will make you nourishment for other people."[5] Consider where you have been through the fire. The tenderization process sensitizes you to specific needs around you, giving you direction concerning your ministry. We minister best in the areas where we have become vulnerable, experienced, and broken. You will receive considerable understanding of an additional mission in life from that question alone.

Let me illustrate with examples from a couple of better-known people at the turn of the twenty-first century:

Charles Colson of Watergate fame (mid-1970s) is actually perceived as the leader in prison ministries. He came to Christ in prison. At the lowest point of his life, God was making a man, crafting a vision, and creating a ministry mission. Since Chuck Colson embraced this brokenness as an index of his primary service, he could see a future vision that would "fit" with his tenderness toward the world—God's Vision.

Joni Eareckson Tada "boasts" a quadriplegic life. I might have said that she is "confined and condemned" to a wheelchair, except that under God she has turned her scar into a vision for service. A broken neck in a swimming accident did not deter her spirit. She can't comb her hair or brush her teeth, but she runs an organization that ministers to the physically disadvantaged of the world. From scar to ministry vision to another dimension of personal mission!

Numerous stories mimic the "scar to ministry vision to personal mission" process—both in secular and Christian voluntarism.

A fourth dimension to life mission will arise from discerning personal vision. Families who lose their kids in drunk driver lunacy feel the pain enough to join "don't drink and drive" campaigns. Those afflicted by cancer set up foundations to find relief and a cure so others might not have to suffer. Women who experience the trauma of abortion while asserting personal freedoms and private rights become vociferous opponents of abortion rights. I could speak about some of the great social reformers of the twentieth century: Mahatma Gandhi, Martin Luther King Jr., Mother Teresa, and Nelson Mandela.

While atheists experience scars and may run to rebellious despair, countless morally informed non-Christians respond to the needs of the world that apply to them.[6] The Christian, too, lives in the present, building on the past and working toward the future. So what makes this process distinct for the Christian? What distinguishes the Christian from the non-Christian in the "scar to ministry to mission" process is the interpretation and perspective placed on the experience.

Differing worldviews accent time differently. The dominant Eastern view looks back to the past as the determining element. The past carries explanatory power, though some people use it as an excuse for indolence in the present. Focusing on the past can also lock people in a prison, especially if they believe in victimizing, unbreakable karmic law. The past explains, but it should not tie us down there. The Western worldview focuses on creating the future. Unfortunately, many live in "dream time," in a series of broken dreams. The future draws us to it, but we should not live in it. That's like looking forward to graduation day without studying for today's exam. Or to put it another way, the windshield needs to be bigger than the rearview mirror, but both are needed for the journey. Neither replaces the need for intentional driving. The past and future are only critical as they influence the present. The present is now. It draws from the past and receives from the future. The biblical view of the future backs into it. Your past has shaped you, but you are not determined by it. Your future calls you, but you cannot predict it. So you live in the here and now, with one eye to the past and the other to future. Without both eyes, your present view will be flawed.

A Christian interpretation of the "scar" points to God— His no-mistake governance, His creation of a personal ministry, His large vision to bring people to Himself, and His philosophy and methodology of ministry to people. A close friend and accountability partner of mine, Tony Evans, has become a well-known proponent for inner-city transformation, having been affected by the despondency of his own inner-city experiences. He wants to build cities from the "inside out"—a distinctly Christian conversion sentiment. Howard Hendricks, first my professor and now a colleague at Dallas Theological Seminary, was deeply scarred by a childhood experience of parental divorce. He has been a leading voice on marriage and ardently promotes a growing relationship between spouses and God as the only way to a growing relationship between them—a truly biblical paradigm for service.

My own service-directing scars arose during virulent adolescence in southern India. My father left a rather lucrative job in an already poor economy and took a vocational Christian worker's position. The 75 percent cut in his salary affected my clothing, my friends, and even my food quality! Without that tenderization process, however, I wouldn't have been sensitive to the needs of Christian workers in weaker economies. Today I have the joy of transferring hundreds of thousands of dollars worth of skills, tools, and resources to pastoral leaders in poorer nations. God was working out a ministry toward His Vision that I would eventually embrace as a mission in life.

Only when your heart is broken is there power, direction, and commitment to a personal vision as your mission in life. That is a "calling" in the biblical sense. Properly responded to, pain creates the atmosphere for submission, and if trained in righteousness, finds sources and resources for service (Heb. 12:1ff.). A calling is when the Vision of bringing people to God takes on a unique personal dimension, a specific role for your life, and a perceivable direction for immediate attention. What you want to do with this mission in the future is your personal vision. What you see being done with your broken, tested, and humbled life to change the lives of others who go through similar types of experiences turns into part of your personal vision. Yet God's "firing" work is not over when we simply discern our personal vision.

Chambers observes:

> [God] gives us a vision, and then He takes us down to the valley to batter us into the shape of that vision. It is in the valley that so many of us give up and faint. . . . While still in the light of the glory of the vision we go right out to do things, but the vision is not yet

real in us. God has to take us into the valley and put us through fires and floods to batter us into shape, until we get to the point where He can trust us with the reality of the vision. Ever since God gave us the vision, He has been at work.[7]

We can't simply talk about a vision without participating in it. Ongoing suffering in accomplishing the Vision tests our commitment to it. That's why we so often want to give up.

When you process your past, you find indices toward how you fulfill your life. You may want to ignore your past, not listen to its noise or relive its pain, but you'll find mission-critical pointers there. Indeed, as much as you want to suppress the noise, God will supervise its assertion into personal attention and action. I introduced the Star-Scar Sketching exercise at a company luncheon, and a young lady made her way to the front after the meeting. In the victorious tone of a Greek *eureka* moment, she realized her calling. Having had six different men in the role of "dad" in the first nineteen years of her existence was no joke. The "scar to ministry" model immediately gave her direction. She said, "Now I know why I went through that hell. So I can be of help to kids from broken homes!" That became her ministry life of service—the fourth dimension of her mission in life—in addition to personal, family, and work life. What was her personal vision? To bless kids from broken homes at her local church. She immediately put some goals and action plans in place: (1) By Sunday, speak to the pastor about her availability in this specific area of need in the children's ministry; (2) work with the Director of Christian Education at church to come up with a specialized ministry of comfort for children from broken families by the end of the school year;

(3) find appropriate materials and resources for this ministry; and (4) start the program in early September.

Three great advantages concerning our passion, priorities, and our "pulpits" lie in the "scar to ministry to mission" process. Let's look at these more closely.

Concentrated Passion

As said before, passion carries "hard" connotations—loving God with all you've got—but also "soft" ones in the realms of life. Of course, we can mistake the soft passions for valid hard ones and go after them with great zeal. What should simply beckon us as missions in life—personal, family, and work life—demand great energy and resources. If you add "ministry life" to those missions, that dimension too needs some of your overflow passion. But where would you receive the overflow passion for the ministry dimension? You could arouse this passion from a heightened awareness of people's needs. Except I know I get preoccupied with other matters at hand. Today, my car needs an oil change, my kid's keyboard needs to be returned, three "urgent" files require attention this afternoon, and alas the day is done!

To keep soft passion alive toward the specific kind of needs I can meet requires an "aliveness" of the scars we have suffered. I must implement a way to keep the scars and what they mean alive. For me, I do this through ministry travel. Unless I am exposed to needs in an ongoing manner, my heart gets hard. An academic environment keeps my mind alive, but unfortunately it hardens my heart. Ministry travel helps my heart to remain sensitive, soft, and supple. Tenderness and kindness, attendant emotions to Christian compassion, supposedly go against *machismo*, but it is Christlike to be broken. It is all right to weep over the world, to show emotion.

On one trip to war-torn, strife-ridden, economically broken Liberia, eleven hundred pastoral leaders (including two hundred pastors' wives and women pastors) sat through nine hours a day of teaching. On the final night, a thousand certificates and books were given out to the delegates. It took a long time, and it seemed longer in the muggy heat without fans or air conditioning. I was worn out, but here came a group of men wanting to talk to me.

"We are twenty-two men needing money to go home tonight."

My responsibility oriented questions kicked in, "Why? What happened? Didn't you plan for it?"

They replied, "Yes, we did. But we used it up in coming to the conference every day."

I asked, "How much does it cost?"

"Three dollars each on the bus," they replied.

"How much can you contribute toward that ticket?" I said, thinking to myself: *How wonderfully sharp am I going to be when faced with immediate human need? The bus fare for some of these men is a third of their monthly income. Don't I like to go home on the first flight after I finish a conference? Won't I help them go home right away?*

Just then an older man stepped to the front. Not many older men were left in Liberia at that time, for the forty-to-sixty-year age bracket had been wiped out during the civil war. It suddenly felt like my dad was asking me, his son, for three dollars to go home, and to take his friends along with him. That moment broke the scab around my heart. It bled again.

Unless I place myself near human need, I am not going to keep the "scar to ministry to mission" process alive. God doesn't want a sympathy that leaves after seeing the images, a tear that is wiped away with a paper napkin and dropped in the wastebasket. He wants the images and experiences of personal deprivation to stir me to do something significant to meet the emergency needs of pastoral leaders in weaker economies. My brokenness empowers my concentration. In fact, this concentration becomes the "burden" component of my calling.

Scar-based ministry helps you focus on this additional mission in the middle of daily pressures. This also means that those who have not been broken will be less susceptible to service opportunities. The safer the life, the less inclined to minister specifically. The richer the economy and the safer the environment, the fewer the radical servants of God. Think of the obverse, and now you know why millions of Christian leaders are emerging in the weaker economies of the world. Broken by scars and needs, they are possessed and burdened to do something. And they are going at it with great zeal, unswervingly committed to a vision to change lives at great sacrifice. Having experienced pain, they are neither immune to the pains of others nor afraid of future pain themselves. I asked a youth pastor who had been physically beaten how he felt about serving Jesus. He meekly but boldly assured me that now that he had gone through the experience, he wasn't afraid anymore!

I've also found that our willingness to take risks in ministry connects with our experience of pain in the past. If you want to live a risk-free, pain-free life, you are doomed to chasing the safe life. However, the fact that you have suffered, moaned, and mourned in your past allows you to be enterprising and courageous for God. Your personal challenge will lie not in discovering vision for mission but in avoiding the presumption and recklessness of justifying anything you want to do based on past experience of pain. This self-examination keeps you from a passive and reactive life, consuming it on your own lusts. Should a person who isn't bold be called a leader? Would a person who doesn't take risks pursue a personal vision and mission? Scar-based ministry allows you to live by faith in the God who trusted you with those scars, and in whom you trusted during the scarring process.

Critical Priorities

Thousands of needs surround us. We can't do much about most of them, but that doesn't mean that we should do nothing about any of them. For a start, your scars enable you to distinguish between *needs* and *opportunities*. I remember a student who said that his scars related to the fact that "my dad didn't play ball with me!" He wrote this paper twenty years after he had left home, and his relationship with his dad was still raw. You know what kind of needs he would notice. Yet scars allow you to move from sensitivities to strategic priorities—again the "burden" that you carry in life.

How do we discern strategic priorities for our ministry vision? One of the factors in the filtering process from needs to opportunities relates to personal scars. Other factors include the gifts and resources that God has given to us. Our sensitivities to particular kinds of needs arise from those dark nights we spent tasting the salt in our tears. It is no wonder that converted drug addicts pursue those caught in the locked vices of addiction in spite of a million other needs surrounding them. We'll look at other factors in strategic prioritizing in the opportunity filter below.

Credible Pulpits

A scar-based ministry also provides credibility in your involvement. I am presently trying to help a couple in the throes of divorce. I would like to get their attention (bash each one's self-centeredness with a baseball bat because several families are being destroyed), dialogue with them, and get them to talk. I have talked with them individually, but they are not talking to each other. They give ear to me, but in the back of the husband's mind is the refrain, "Listen to this guy, but remember he hasn't gone through divorce so he doesn't really understand me." When I counsel from God's Word there is authority, but any insight for wise application can be rejected because I haven't experienced the pain of severe marital conflict myself.

When your service arises from scars and your vision is to change lives with similar scars, credibility attends you. How would Joni Eareckson Tada be received if she weren't physically handicapped? And Chuck Colson if he hadn't been to prison? If I hadn't experienced the constraints of a Christian worker's family in a weaker economy? We might be received politely, even appreciatively, but not eagerly or openheartedly. People want somebody who has walked in their shoes and lived inside their skins. They can accept such a person for credible ministry.

Be certain, however, that you have been "trained" by suffering before you turn weakness into service. I heard of a leader of the SADD (Students Against Drunk Driving) movement who was himself convicted of drinking and driving. When asked how he could be against drunk driving and still drink and drive, his lawyer argued that he was against drunk driving when he was sober! Obviously, they had the wrong leader. He did not possess a credible pulpit for his crusade.

Jack Perry, my father-in-law, lived the last five years of his life struggling with cancer. He functioned as a hospital chaplain in the latter period of his life after serving for decades in the pastorate. An ardent personal evangelist, he brought many in hospitals to the Savior. Talk about scar-based ministry! A hero of the first kind to the rest of our family, he turned the scar of terminal disease into a personal ministry vision—introducing people on sickbeds to the Lord Jesus. He never missed work until his final week. He visited many other patients with terminal illness. When we went to visit Papa Jack, he would take me along on his chaplain rounds. I remember meeting Mr. Lundgren in his home, now confined to a wheelchair. Dad asked me to pray at the end of the visit. My prayer rang hollow because I didn't know the reality of suffering with cancer. Mr. Lundgren accepted my pious prayer graciously, but he and Pastor Jack resonated more deeply. Why? Jack Perry carried focused death in his own body. No one dared to say him, "But you don't know what it is to feel pain, anticipate death, or experience grief." Jack would tell his own story. It was no wonder so many trusted Christ from their hospital beds. A personal vision arising from the scar of deep illness turned into ministry—an added mission to his life and became his burden for the rest of his life. With God's help, you too can be open to the scars-to-ministry opportunities in your life.

Processing Your Present—A Resource Inventory

A baby camel asked his mother, "Mom, why do I have these huge three-toed feet?"

His mother replied, "To help you stay on the top of the soft sand while trekking across the desert."

"Why long eyelashes?"

"To keep the sand out of your eyes on our trips through the desert."

"Why humps?"

"To store water for our long treks across the desert."

Crusoe is a man on a small rock with a few comforts just snatched from the sea; the best thing in the book is simply the list of things saved from the wreck. The greatest poem is an inventory.

G. K. CHESTERTON

'That's great, Mom. We have huge feet to stop us from sinking, long eyelashes to keep sand out of our eyes, and humps to store water. But, Mom . . . "

"Yes, son?"

"Why are we in the zoo?"

We've looked at the past, learning that we can't live in or for it. Now that you've sketched the past, I'd like you to audit the present. Commence a study of your *present* life by taking a personal inventory. The baby camel inventoried his resources.

discovered the reasons for his endowments, and asked the right question of his mother. We will acknowledge our resources and their reasons; then we shall be unleashed into God's Vision.

What do you presently hold in your hand that will help direct your involvement in the Vision? Again, this process of discovery and execution requires thoughtful reflection and periodic reviews. As I edit this work, I am coming off a monthlong atmosphere of personal reexamination, culminated by a two-day spontaneous time for replenishment and reinforcement of God's work and calling in my life. I encourage you to assign an undisturbed segment of time, perhaps a day, for personal life exegesis. Otherwise, you will while away your life. You won't know how to appropriately use the time you save through rigorous time management!

We are looking at vision-specific issues so you can fulfill your personal vision under God's Vision for the world. There are two sides to the ledger of your present: resources and opportunities. On the resource side of your ledger fall your gifts, temperament, seasons of life, and other resources such as talents, education, family, friends, finances, as well as your interests, connections, and even hobbies. On the opportunity side, you will observe needs and arenas for your involvement. Resources and opportunities go together. Opportunities show direction for life investment. Identifying your resources will help you define the *nature* of your investment as well as the *capacity* you bring to fulfill the strategies of your vision and God's Vision.

GIFT RESOURCES INVENTORY

Allow me to briefly expand on the list I provided above, giving you some idea of the particular areas you must assess and inventory.

Gifts

I am not referring to your natural skills and talents, for those will predominate in your profession and occupation. Your spiritual gifts, however, enable you in your service—the personal ownership of God's Vision as mission in your life. Of course, the more your skills, talents, and gifts coincide with each other and with opportunities that God creates, the more fruitful and fulfilling life is.

Your spiritual gifts could be one in number or a bundle. As in most spiritual areas, more is not necessarily better; more just means more responsibility. Four passages in Scripture delineate spiritual gifts: Romans 12; 1 Corinthians 12–14; Ephesians 4; 1 Peter 4. Peter broadly classified the gifts he listed into speaking gifts and serving gifts. Disagreement on the number of spiritual gifts, continuation of certain gifts, and whether the lists are exhaustive sends me to this broad but biblical distinction.[1] Spiritual gifts that reflect the glory of God in edifying and expanding the body of Christ fall within the biblical division of "speaking" and "serving" gifts.

How does one go about discovering spiritual giftedness? May I suggest four basic criteria for your gift-discernment process?

The Criterion of Recognition

Recognition by others is extremely important because we are given to self-delusion. We mistake dreams for visions, wants for facts, desires for realities. It doesn't matter what your gift is, you will be recognized for its effectiveness over time by a cross section of God's people beyond your immediate circle of relationships. If I think I possess the gift of preaching while people consistently fall asleep on me, it doesn't matter what I think—I probably don't have that gift. I know some pastors who regularly exercise the gift of "healing"—healing people of sleeplessness! Find out whether people recognize and respond to your gift. Do they provide unsolicited expressions encouraging you in a certain gift?

Think about this criterion of recognition and who gives you affirmation. The matter becomes crucial in detecting your gifts, especially if you are young in your spiritual walk.

The Criterion of Attraction

Whom do you admire? To which set of people are you drawn? With whom do you share stories of ministry, both successes and failures? To whom do you go for advice? Who has God opened for friendship at this level over the years? You'll find yourself unknowingly, perhaps supernaturally, drawn to the ones who carry similar giftedness. In my early years it was my pastor; in late teenage years it was a team leader; on my first job it was the Bible teacher of the organization; during seminary years it was a particular kind of professor. At present, my accountability partner is someone far more accomplished than I, but who shares similar gifts. My present mentor in his heyday was one of the top five speakers in America.

In the last twenty years I have discovered the gift of giving—"the special ability that God gives certain members of the body of Christ to contribute their material resources to the work of the Lord with liberality and cheerfulness."[2] Some of my closest friends are givers. For twenty years I have received from them, not only materially but also received the best gift of all—the gift of giving.

Putting the two criteria together—recognition and attraction—I am reasonably certain that I possess speaking and giving gifts.

The Criterion of Opportunities

Study the opportunities that God has opened up for the use of your gifts in the last year, last five years, or last ten years. Look especially at the service opportunities that God has created for you. These are the opportunities that you didn't merit, maneuver, or manipulate. After all, God, the Giver of spiritual gifts, will match your gifts with spiritual opportunities. By looking at opportunities, an index to the kind of gifts that you possess will emerge. This morning, I opened up my e-mail to find an invitation to speak at a premier professional society within my discipline. I am still praying about whether I should take it for reasons of time commitments, but that doesn't negate the fact that only God could have opened up the opportunity. I didn't seek the opportunity, neither did I even think of it. One of the choicest of God's senior homileticians who had been given the spot canceled at the last moment, and now the opportunity has fallen to me.

These opportunities may be desired but neither sought nor created by you. A television time buyer for Christian programs contacts the head of media at a sister organization about getting on international Christian television. The media producer declines the invitation but asks if a Christian speaker—referring to me—can be placed on prime time, *secular* television on New Year's Day 2000. "Impossible," responds the time buyer, "it's not been done in history." The conversation ends. Two months later he contacts the producer with a prime-time slot, on the largest secular television network in the world. You may remember January 1, 2000 with its media hype and personal fear combined in the approaching Y2K. The psychological odometer of the human race changed triple zeroes with twenty-four-hour programming from across the world as capital cities marked midnight. That day became the biggest television-watching day in history! Our ministry *RREACH* International had less than two months to raise seed money, produce the program, buy airtime, get the program approved, and advertise the event. I was addressing the English-speaking, Internet-connected audience of the world—our screening filters to define "opinion leaders." It was accomplished in less than a sixth of the cost and an eighth of the time that large organizations cautioned us it would take. God gave the proclamation gifts, provided the human, monetary, and technological resources. But most important, God opened an unprecedented opportunity to reach tens (perhaps hundreds) of millions of people in nearly one hundred countries. Our organization's slogan has turned into an operational value: "ONLY GOD." The opportunity indexed the gift.

You can also read opportunities from another angle. What opportunities has God given for you to *develop* your gift? What opportunities have you seized in becoming better in your service for the Lord? These are ancillary and circular, for as you seize opportunities that have opened up, you will either find confirmation or negation in your gifting.

By the way, many Christians experience self-doubt concerning their giftedness. Most in my profession do. I know I do. I especially wonder when I watch or listen to a tape of a sermon I did. I cannot get over why anybody would come to hear me at all, why anybody would say they benefited from a certain talk is beyond me. Doubt about your giftedness helps your humility quotient in the face of exaggerated affirmation. Doubt calls for areas of gift development. I used to speak too fast to be understood and had to slow down. Doubt enables your reliance on God before an opportunity. However, when you're in self-defeating doubt about your gift, you will find that these unexplainable opportunities confirm the gifts that God has given you. I often have to assure myself that God would not have opened up unsought opportunities if not for some measure of giftedness already present.

The Criterion of Satisfaction

The least objective of the discovery criteria, nevertheless important, is the satisfaction you receive in exercising your gift. You can find out about your satisfied giftedness in the following ways:

1. *Check your Star Sketch (from chap. 8). What are the high points of your ministry accomplishments?*

   If you read my Star Sketch, you would find a Bolivian event where two-thirds of the stadium walked forward at the evangelistic invitation, a family camp opportunity where all known nonbelievers trusted Christ, and several pastors' conferences where God liberated pastoral leaders in the areas of preaching, living, and thinking biblically. My Star Sketch reveals my joy, satisfaction, and delight in a pattern of similar speaking engagements. This reveals evangelistic and teaching gifts.

2. *Where do you sense God's satisfaction from your life? What goes beyond your own satisfaction to a sense of God's joy? When do you sense God's pleasure?*[3]

   I remember sensing God's joy when I was in the country of Chad—a most economically broken piece of the world. The leading pastor's home was a clay hut. Our hosts took us to the only spot near N'Djamena, the capital city, where the gospel had never been presented. They gave me an open-air speaking opportunity using a sound system that barely worked. I preached with two simultaneous translations being made in the dominant languages. While the process was tedious— think of multiplying my lengthy sermons by three and you'll find it tiresome just thinking about it—I still sensed God's pleasure in all my tiredness. At the invitation, a few started stirring. One or two came to the front. My hosts asked me to step aside to let their own men give the invitation in their native tongues. A dozen local leaders got up and took turns speaking to the people in their own languages about Jesus, the exclusive Mediator between God and all humanity. As they invited fellow citizens of another religion and various languages to trust the Savior, my eyes filled with tears as my soul overflowed with joy. I knew that God was pleased with this international, multiracial, multilingual response. And they came forward! Two hundred of them. God was pleased with the execution of His Vision, and I was pleased with God's pleasure.

Keep in mind, however, that "results" do not necessarily reveal gifting. Many of God's servants have to work in the most difficult places at great expense with few quantifiable results, especially in evangelism. Results may reveal the effectiveness of a program, but there are many variable factors. Actually, I'd rather count responses—business discipline calls for measurement but not results—some of which may not be known for decades or even until eternity. In ministry, results do not necessarily reveal the effectiveness of the person or the project, just the efficiencies. That effectiveness comes from knowing that God's pleasure rests on them as they minister from their giftedness, regardless of the results. Indeed, my responsibility is to seize opportunities of scale and leave the scope to God.

3. *What do you desire in ministry? What are you burdened about?*

I use the word *burden* in the sense of Paul's stewardship of his gifts (Eph. 3:7–8), his sense of obligation (Rom. 1:14), and his sworn-oath mentality (1 Tim. 2:7). I am speaking of "sanctified" desire for the glory of God, the extension of His salvation, and the building up of the church. Since even ministry motives can be mixed, you will have to spend time in dialogue with God, Scripture, and accountability partners. Your ministry desires can reveal your giftedness and help you articulate a visionary burden for your life. Do you carry a specific kind of burden in ministry? Your burden arises from a matrix interaction of needs, resources, and opportunities.

At the present time, I am not burdened to serve the AIDS-infested communities of the world. Not because I don't desire to serve the sick, tired, poor, and dying. I am willing to, especially if they are geographically close to me as part of my Christian responsibility. But this service option does not arise because my present burdens arise from spiritual giftedness in other areas. My spiritual giftedness aligns with a burden to evangelize the opinion leaders and strengthen the pastoral leaders of the world who, in turn, live in and can influence AIDS-infested regions. I am occupied with ways in which those leaders can be reached. Why are these the primary ministry desires, the main burdens of my life? Well, ministry desires and burdens parallel ministry gifts.

4. *Where are your ministry frustrations? Where do people critique you? Where are you weak?*

On the obverse side of ministry desires lie the frustrations in ministry that would be addressed by God's resources. For instance, I dislike reading financial statements and discussing salary plans in board meetings. Who cares about those? Ask me to speak about vision in ministry, not manage people or administer details. My office wants me to have my speaking notes to them a week before a meeting because it throws them into confusion to receive them at the last minute. I clearly don't understand or sympathize with the administrative process. I have gotten better at it, but I don't foresee the day when I won't be making last-minute adjustments to PowerPoint presentations. While I feel terrible for their frustration, I also feel bad about mine. Fortunately, even frustrations can guide me in my understanding of spiritual gifts—at least in what they are not.

Take this grid of criteria—recognition, attraction, opportunities, and satisfaction—and sift your lists through them to come up with single or multiple giftings. It doesn't mean that you are limited to one kind of gift or giftedness. God may change, add, and grow gifts in your life that you never thought of before. Giftedness also doesn't mean that you don't have responsibilities in other areas of service. Timothy may not have been gifted as an evangelist, but he had to "do the work of an evangelist" (2 Tim. 4:5).

Finally, acknowledge the Giver of the gift when you are granted favor and success. Do not confuse His favor with your greatness, for the *gift* is larger than the *person*.[4] You must come to understand how God has gifted you so that you can fulfill a personal calling within the Vision, which is bigger than both gift and person.

Temperament

After studying your giftedness, the next category to investigate in processing personal, present resources is the study of your temperament. I find great frustration among gifted people because they don't understand their temperaments. Personality traits can cancel out great giftedness. Our schools graduate incredibly gifted people who cannot work with the people among whom they must exercise their gifts.

We need to understand our temperamental types just to be welcomed, let alone be effective. For instance, I draw energy from being with people; an associate draws energy from computers. It is better, then, that my gifts are exercised with people than with computers. Computers test my sanctification all the time; people test his. I am a bit more patient with people; he is very patient with computers.

We also need to discern temperaments to allow for and accept differences—an opportunity to apply the virtue of Christian love. People are different, really different. I make decisions differently than an associate of mine. Reversible decisions—where to eat out tonight—are made quickly. I take longer times on irreversible decisions, but not as long as he does. Practically, I have worked out the 30/70 principle of decision making. I make bad decisions if I have less than 30 percent of the information and delay decisiveness if I don't possess 70 percent of the information I need. Of course, I can't wait until all the information becomes available to me—that's asking for near omniscience. How do I tell what percentage of the information I have? That knowledge comes from experience, which turns into wisdom in the specific details of life. It also comes from giving weight to the decision. Deciding where to go out to eat tonight is not as weighty as determining whom you should marry. Eating out only requires 30 percent of the information (do you have money to eat out? what is your family's preference?). Whom you should marry, on the other hand, asks for information about the kind of person the potential spouse is. Is she a believer? Is she a growing believer? What are his focuses in life? His upbringing? Her family background? Gaining that information requires more deliberation—and you'd better be working toward knowing 70 percent of that person before you walk down the aisle. But don't plan to wait until you have 100 percent of the information, because you never will! Accepting personality differences not only allows you some freedom in the big decisions; it helps you put up with, work with, and enjoy the ones you choose. I am speaking here of temperaments that enable you in your service, not mere psychological profiling. But you need to know your temperament so you can pursue a personality-compatible vision.[5]

Self-understanding will help you know how you make decisions, what motivates you, what burns you out, what rewards you need and desire, how you want to be managed, your behavior under stress, and especially how you learn. Please take all this with a grain of salt, however. Every one of these tests attempts to place you in molds and averages. Remember that they generalize; you are unique. The good news here, of course, is that you are not stuck in your "personality" or "temperament." You can know your dominant traits and their weaknesses. But God is able to change your dominant temperament over time with new factors and experiences should He deem that necessary for new utility for Him.

Seasons

What season of life are you in? God's drama includes life cycles that all of us must go through. Fred Smith Sr. my mentor still at eighty-eight, who has passed through nearly all seasons that are possible, pointed out the importance of understanding life's seasons and each one's uniqueness. Seasons come to go; they are not cyclical like annual seasons. The parents of young children live in a different season than when the children are off on their own. At present, our family clearly discerns a different season. We hardly see each other during the week because everyone is busy with different activities. It is imperative, therefore, that we make our weekends count. Consequently, I have cut down on 75 percent of my weekend travel. I leave for Ukraine this Sunday afternoon and hope to come back the following Saturday in order to catch at least one weekend day with the kids—though it costs more money to do that. Each season carries uniqueness about it.

You can better understand your season by mixing your chronological age with people's trust in your influence. Chronological age is not an indicator of spiritual maturity or life experience. As you know, a person who claims to have "ten years of experience" may have had ten years of experience or simply one year's experience each year for ten years. The former has matured beyond chronological aging. Age doesn't guarantee wisdom either; age only shows birthdays. You might as well count in dog years! But some passages of life show discernible, general features.[6] That is, a man who is older is probably better able to handle certain challenges, if he has benefited from earlier experience. However, no one should look down on youth simply because a person is young. A wise young man will contribute more than an old fool. (One of my relatives by marriage decided to leave his wife of more than fifty years to pursue a young beauty. He was seventy-five years old at the time. He had grown in age but not in character or maturity.)

To identify decisive moments for the seasons of your life, look for milestones. Milestones, as you know, dot the road and reveal the passing of time and space. You have finished X number of moments and covered X distance. Boundary markers or transitional times disclose decisive events that launch new chronological seasons in your life. Milestone moments enable self-discovery, while crossroads may help you make ministry discoveries. Turning points differ from milestones in that the road takes a turn and helps you discern God's new leadership in your life. Once you take the turn, you can look back to see that the turn was more than a turning point; it was a crossroad. Looking back, you know that the correct turns were divinely promoted. Even wrong turns were divinely permitted and will be used by God for His purposes.

Just as nature's seasons develop each year, so four seasons roughly frame each life—Foundation, Definition, Implementation, and Conclusion. Advertisements may have many things wrong, but this one thing they have right—you only go around once in the seasons of life. Though there are no guarantees of full life expectancy, each of these seasons represents about a quarter of life, twenty or so years in wealthier economies.

Foundation involves birth and adolescence, early formative experiences. The standard educational course comes in this time period.

Definition includes specialized education, establishment of one's own home, early ministry experiences.

Implementation involves a settling in for primary missions in life (personal, family, work), additionally informed by the ministry vision one has developed or assimilated in the earlier seasons.

Conclusion is that period that can also be active, but at a different pace than previous seasons.

Hopefully these time frames can be useful to you as an outline to fill and fulfill your assignment. I like the Spanish word *estaciónes,* which covers both "seasons" and "stations" in life. While "season" emphasizes change and transition, "station" underscores the constants during the seasons. For example, we need to live *in* the present (steady in "station") but not live *for* the present (anticipating a new "season"). We ought not to live *in* the future (not yet in that "station"), but we may live for a future season.

What about one's roles in understanding life's seasons or stations? Earlier in my life I needed to be a "practitioner." I had to put in the hours, pay my dues as it were, before the Lord placed the mantle of "influencer" on me. That is, I "do" by "influencing" others to do what I used to do! I hope I never stop being a practitioner, but there will probably come a time when I cannot break physical laws anymore—like travel to the Far East for a weekend of ministry, speak within twenty minutes of arrival, return home, and teach the next day. At some point I will have to add an extra day or two at each end for recuperation! Further, I have gone from mere function to occupying a role that people have placed on me. People don't simply want me to be a leader; they want me to be *seen* as a leader! A generous haberdasher provides me fine clothes because he thinks that without his assistance I easily qualify for the title,

"Best dressed by an auto parts store." With his clothing advice, he has helped me to fulfill my God-given role.

As you grow older, and hopefully wiser, people will gain trust in your abilities, character, and leadership. Now comes the question: Will you accept the role that they expect you to play in this new season? Accepting the role that God creates for you is not creating a *persona* around yourself. I find some people involved in persona creation—fake, celebrity minded, self-absorbed, image making. Role acceptance is not so much to pander to others fawning over you but to authentically live the implications of your vision. Billy Graham has carried that role well. He is an evangelist at heart with a Bible in hand. He always wanted to do that. However, God placed a mantle of leadership that rallied itinerant evangelists around the world to his call. He knew the season of his life.

The principal of a theological college in central Europe contemplated a question with me. At age fifty-four, he wondered if he should pursue a doctorate. "I don't have the time to invest in academic preparation anymore," he told me. The "time" word alerted me to the "season" issue. We were able to settle the question quickly. I asked him, "What is your vision—to become an instructor in New Testament studies or to provide theological leadership to the fledgling evangelical church in your country?" Without question, it was the latter. Settled in this decision, he decided not to get his doctorate but instead invested his time in putting together an excellent planning document for his institution.

To discern your role in God's Vision, understand your seasons, value them, and translate them into Christian realities. Whatever happens, don't force seasons! Let God create your seasons, even features abnormal to them, just like He does in nature every year.

OTHER RESOURCES

For the most part, this section on "other resources" will relate to your vocation, and hence to your mission of glorifying God. For some of you, however, there will be compatibility between these other resources and your ministry lives. I do not want to overlook the valuable advantage of personal resources coming to bear on your personal vision.

Talents

Talents (as opposed to spiritual gifts, which are described above) are abilities given by God to both Christians and non-Christians. Non-Christians possess talents as part of God's investment of common grace in their lives. The world can run better with astute, gifted people—both non-Christians and Christians. I have an excellent non-Christian mechanic who keeps my car running well. A person will not be a better mechanic simply because he is a Christian. He can be a better mechanic as a Christian because of all that Christ brings, but he may not be a better mechanic just because he is a Christian. A non-Christian mechanic may have better automotive knowledge, experience, and tools. Of course, if everything remains equal, I would pick a Christian mechanic because of the virtue of honesty and the possibility of a Christian family relationship that I could share with him. But if the Christian mechanic messes up my vehicle twice in a row, I would suspect his ability at making cars (and the world) run better.

When it comes to a ministry vision, talents could work as the means by which your spiritual gifts are implemented. Talents in music or art are easily used as instruments in a gift of teaching. I also find, however, that God *regularly* uses people outside their *talents*—Matthew the financial wizard wrote one of the Gospels—but only *periodically* uses them outside their *giftedness* for edifying the body of Christ.

Look for the best combination of gifts, talents, and arenas for the best way to grasp and implement your vision. I'd like to call this overlay combination a "platform" for service. Let's say you possess the spiritual gift of teaching and your arena seems to be bereaved families (because you lost your dad when you were young). Let's say you are also a talented mechanic. I see a natural alignment for personal vision. You could use your mechanic platform to gain access to bereaved families with car trouble. You can share Christ with them even as you get those pistons running smoothly. If you can't find easy alignment of your gifts, talents, and arenas, let your vision be oriented around your gift and your vocation around your talent. Look, however, for how God may be creating platforms for your vision in and through your vocation.

I applied this process in my life. I know the cluster of my speaking gifts (prophecy, teaching, evangelism, etc.), the range of my talents (thinking, envisioning, communicating, building relationships, etc.), and the arena of their involvement (evangelizing opinion leaders and strengthening pastoral leaders primarily of weaker economies by preaching, teaching, writing).

Education

Education as part of your personal profile gives you certain advantages in life. Education may be formal, informal, or even nonformal. In formal education, you gain entry-level status along with a few options. If you have a degree, you are more likely to be hired in the beginning. But, if you don't perform well, you will either be frustrated or fired, with both causing pain. So you may need to keep up your educational intensity, continuing in formal education. Most professions provide avenues for being certified and keeping up certification.

Through nonformal education, you can get more knowledge in advancing fields, even though you may not receive an academic diploma. Education opens up jobs for your mission of bringing God glory. It also opens up platforms in combination with your gifts and talents for your personal vision to bring people to God. And do not overlook informal education, which is as critical as the other two kinds of education. I am blessed with three mentors in my life, none of whom have gone to college. My formal education makes me a specialist in a very miniscule area. Life is larger than that small area of expertise. Part of my vision scheme gets fleshed out with practical help from great people whom God has placed in my life in terms of gift, concept, skill, values development, and best of all, wisdom and encouragement.

Family
Your family is a resource to help you fulfill your personal vision. I cannot emphasize the critical role they (especially your spouse) play in making personal vision a reality. I have met many young men who believe their families are a drag on them. Frustrated, they give up too easily on their visions or their marriages. Remember, mission comes before vision. Get your family life healthy so that you can go after your vision. But the vision must come or you will not be spiritually profitable to the Lord. Spiritually profitable Christians grow in mission toward their families and in their visions toward the world.

How can family be a resource for your vision? A primary way is emotionally. This is why you must be careful in your choice (at least 70 percent careful!) of a mate. Many a person's defeat and uselessness come from a spouse who does not stand with him or her in the vision for his or her life. Find out, before you marry, if the "candidate" shares the same values, virtues, and mission. Is he or she open to the vision that God may give you?

You may choose to remain single. Paul believed in an unfettered freedom in attending to the affairs of the Lord (1 Cor. 7:32). Your parents, siblings, and extended family may still be garnered for their part in your vision. Declare your ambition to live the chaste and single life for the vision and you will possibly find empathetic family members who take you on as part of their service to the world. The history of Christian missions is marked by singles who made a profound contribution to the march of God among many nations.

If married, however, don't drop either spouse or vision. Instead, pray, study, and find God's will together. You would want to do the Star-Scar Sketch separately and share your past. One couple did the sketch and communicated their joys and hurts, their pride and humiliation, their high and low points, and remarked: "We've been married eleven years and we found out stuff about each other for the first time." You may then do the Resource-Opportunity Inventory together. Look for the other's perceptions of your resources and talk. Work through the needs-to-opportunities filter (chapters 9 and 10) together. It is amazing how you can come to harmonious conclusions on these mission-critical and vision-critical matters. Then see if you can provide chances for the other to grow in areas of your sensitivities, priorities, and strategies. Find out which vision dominates and enable each other to its fulfillment.

My wife knew from the beginning that if she married me, she would have to put up with my peripatetic lifestyle of extensive travel. Fortunately, God prepared her for these kinds of absences with her pastor-father, who was also busy in his work. She is not a traveler—her interests do not lie in getting on a plane and crossing oceans. But we are united in this endeavor. She doesn't merely *let* me go on trips. Even though there is pain over separation, she *sends* me with her love to the world. She has resolved in her life that her role is different than mine in our joint vision for the world. She also knows that the safest place for me to be is in God's will.

When you think of family, think also of your extended family as a resource. What does your heritage bring to your mission? How have your parents and grandparents set the course of your life? On my father's side are five generations of ministers. I couldn't escape the ministry! My children receive a slant toward their vision and mission from both sets of truly grand grandparents.

Depending on your culture and family systems, you want to think of your responsibilities to siblings as well. Are there ways you can cultivate extended family into your vision? After all, family businesses exist on every part of the planet. Why not family visions in God's great Vision?

Your family is not a burdensome annoyance. They are the brakes that God has sovereignly placed in your life so you won't hit the embankment at full speed. You can get them traveling in the same vehicle with you through prayer and vision casting. They can be the greatest emotional resource for your ministry vision if you cultivate and include them in your personal mission. As our second son headed into his senior year in high school, he became interested in going to a most distressed part of the world—the Ethiopia-Somalia border. The vision seems to have caught on. I will wait to see how it works out over the long term.

Friends

Friends are a resource from the Lord for your vision, even as you function in their vision for the Lord. God brings people around you all the time. They fit within emotional circles of relationship. Some will develop into inner-circle buddies. Hopefully, your spouse is in that circle. Your prayer and accountability partner(s) would uninhibitedly locate themselves in the inner sanctum. You wouldn't mind them dropping into your life without setting up prior appointments. You like their interruptions. They fight the fight and run the race alongside you.

Your middle level can be counted on in emergencies and times of personal need. They wish you well. They know that God's hand is on you in this particular vision and want to express regular support—emotionally, spiritually, and financially. Like doctors, they are available on call. Often, they'll stand by until you really need their life participation.

All others would find themselves in the outer circles of friendship—the circle of acquaintance. (You wouldn't place anyone outside the outer circle—enemies place themselves there.) For the most part, these acquaintances don't run the race with you. You gain resources for your vision from your inner and middle circles, while acknowledging that some will move in and others move out of the circles. Time and other constraints limit most friendships.

Don't forget that friends bring along their friends—your network from which you find friends. When net worth is evaluated by network, you'll soon find an arena of influence beyond your wildest dreams. The entire network can be informed about your vision, with some of them recruited by your acquaintances for the greater cause.

Friendships are found at peer level but also among those older or younger than you. Most friendships begin naturally (or really supernaturally) but must be developed intentionally. The only intention I have in showing attention to friends is to develop them for the Vision, whether they buy into *my* vision or not. Before long, however, everyone associated who cares for relational proximity with me will be confronted with the question of whether they are going to get on board in some manner with the vision that God has given to me. Many are threatened by my activities, others are amazed, and some risk their involvement. I intentionally nurture inner-circle relationships; the middle circle is left to a more passive cultivation; while the rest are left to "providential luck"! I believe that I would be wasting the stewardship of the lives that have been placed in my inner and middle circle if I didn't give them the opportunity to participate with me and all the while giving them the freedom to move away.

Finances

Finally, don't forget your monetary resources. Since we've said much about money in these books—the final competitor for deification in many a contemporary life—all I ask here is a view of money that doesn't hold tight to its fleeting advantages. Instead, make your money become a powerful resource to implement your burden. Biblical "channeling" holds everything with open palms as an instrument to fund the vision. Just before I addressed a gathering of Christian philanthropists, a young Englishman shared his definition of a millionaire: "I will be a millionaire when I give away a million pounds for the Lord's work worldwide. The mission of my company is to be a financial resource for the kingdom." I don't think anyone listened to my talk after that Copernican perspective shift in the definition of "millionaire" that decentered their money mindedness. Now who wants to be a millionaire?

Processing Your Present—An Opportunity Inventory

An IQ test question asks: "A man walked all the way from Dublin to Cork along main roads without passing a single pub. How did he man-

> *Some reporters said I don't have any vision. I don't see it.*
>
> —PRESIDENT GEORGE H. W. BUSH

age that, since there are many pubs in Ireland?" Answer: "He did not pass a single pub. He went into every one of them!"

Millions of needs surround us. Thousands of crises beck-on our attention. I frequently see two responses, neither of which is particularly effective in meeting human need. Spiritually growing Christians can easily be seduced by the needs into attempting the impossible without clear direction or real impact. They try to meet every need in some way. I find this scattering of personal services with a smattering of resources especially among Christians in weaker economies who strive to serve the Lord Jesus. I so admire their eagerness and do not doubt their spiritual maturity the least bit. I has-ten to humbly ask questions about the use of their resources. Often their missions in life—personal, family, and work—get neglected in the press of the ministry.

Yet, there is another set of Christians, infantile and

hard-hearted, who steel themselves against world needs under the slogan that "the need is not the call." Just because they can't do much about most needs, they do nothing about anything. Or as a friend would say it, with a double negative for emphasis, "they don't do nuthin' about nuthin'!" They live in a self-enclosed self-embrace, inside cocoons of comfort, safety zones away from any plausible hardship. At a West Coast zoo, I found (somewhat inappropriately I thought) one of political philosopher Edmund Burke's memorable quotations, "Nobody makes a greater mistake than he who did nothing because he could do only a little." Consequently, we have to move from placating and neglecting any and every need. Here are some guidelines.

FROM NEEDS TO OPPORTUNITIES

How does one select opportunities from a multitude of needs? We can't look on every need as an opportunity like the Irish reveler dropping into every bar. Neither should our practicality turned to callousness keep us from meeting any needs. If the Bible assures us of the impossibility of a totally balanced life on the earth while waiting for a perfect eternity, the better mistake to make is the former one. The first imbalance is more biblical in the hierarchy of God's expectations. It is better to die young and shriveled, having sacrificed your life for the sake of God's Vision, than old and rich, having attempted to gain life on your own. Yes, the need is not the call. The calling must come from above—another distinguishing mark between non-Christian and Christian searches for life vision. If calling depends on needs around you, you will be torn to pieces. I suggest the tactic below to anyone who really wants to serve God with zeal, even though the need in itself is not the opportunity or calling, cause or mandate. We will come to considering strategic burdens soon.

To those who desire to live intentionally but are filled with apathy, recognize that your calling arises in the context of *present* needs. Any human need is potentially a justification for your service. Meeting someone else's need is a starting point for intentional living. One of the spiritual problems of insensitive people is immaturity and vice versa. You need to admit your selfishness, acknowledge your hard-heartedness, and confess your sin to God. Of course, in confession, you are not giving Him private information about you. You are opening up your life in submission for His merciful stimulation of your heart, to soften your crusty insides. You may want to ask Him to create time (again!) in your busyness so you can be involved in His Vision. Remember, God is committed enough to His Vision to have given His one and only Son for it. He will do anything that is necessary if you ask Him to create the resources for your obedience to His Vision.

Ask God also to alert you to human needs, both ultimate and felt needs. The ultimate human need is to become right with God. Felt needs are existentially more real to human beings and cloud their view of the ultimate answer. So you can do something about felt needs as well, with the qualifier that you will meet those needs as a means to introducing people to the ultimate solution to their root need—the Lord Jesus Christ (yet another distinction between Christian and non-Christian versions of calling).

Let me lay out a continuum by which you can filter the plethora of needs around you in order to possibly recognize service opportunities. These four "filtration" stages running between parallel lines of information and emotion will help discern ministry opportunity in the continuum of global need.

OPPORTUNITIES FILTER

INFORMATION

Peripheral Thoughtful Emotional Personal
Awareness Reflection Response Responsibility

EMOTION

Peripheral Awareness: You may have heard of the non-profit board member who remarked, "All this misery, all these wars, and the destruction of the environment. At some point, everyone has to draw his own conclusions and act accordingly. As for me, I've cancelled my subscription to the daily newspaper."[1] If I were even remotely sympathetic to only the front pages of today's newspaper, the following needs would demand my attention:

Hurricane relief efforts

Middle East political tensions

Troubled kids

Drug abuse

AIDS

Homelessness

Unless you are selfish and hard-hearted (that's why your spiritual love for Jesus Christ ought to precede your recognition of needs), you will be peripherally aware of some needs.

Peripheral Awareness involves a low level of information and emotion, but the need has registered on the radar screen of your life.

At that point, I would seriously converse with God, asking Him if I should address any of these needs of which I have become aware. Should I do something immediately about the impact of hurricanes on the coasts? If I lived in Bangladesh, where countless lives are lost each year because of recurring cyclones, I would be aware of such a need. If I were in Zimbabwe and was not aware of the AIDS obituaries, it would mean I have signed off from spirituality. If you are not aware of street children in Lagos or Manila, we have to check your pulse. If you are not aware of racial problems in the United States, wake up.

At the least, *be aware.* And ask God for your role in helping solve the problems of your community, city, country, and the world. In fact, ask Him to widen your vision. He will take on that responsibility for you, as a challenge from you.

Over the years I have had the privilege of speaking to business, government, academic, and professional leaders in the weaker economies of the world. As I became more aware of trends, I found that the leaders from these weaker economies were actually living within the main cities of the United States. They also wield enormous influence back in their home countries. I became aware of immigrant owners of small and large companies, and professionals who staffed the medical and technological facilities in the whole nation. The more I looked, the more I saw them around me, on planes, in airports, at shopping centers. If I hadn't looked for them, I wouldn't have seen them. Matthew says, "When [Jesus] *saw* the crowds" (Matt. 9:36, italic added). This "seeing" is not the exercise of the physical sight. It was more than ogling them with eyeballs. Many needs surround us, but what do you and I see? Really see and feel? Move to the second stage.

Thoughtful Reflection: Of the many needs around you, to which do you find yourself giving a second and third thought? Most likely, information will move ahead of emotion here. You may not be able to identify the reason for your curiosity. The Holy Spirit can instigate your mind as well as your emotions. In the case of the international leaders in the United States, I wondered how they were being reached with the gospel. I knew of some evangelistic activity with political leaders in the Washington, D.C., and New York City areas. About fifty organizations were involved in reaching international students. But there was a gaping hole. No one was intentionally reaching the immigrant or international business professional as a specific ministry.

What captures your second and third thoughts from the panorama of needs these days? Pray about why these few needs stick in your mind.

Emotional Response: Note that the sequence from needs to opportunities runs on the parallel rails of information and emotion. Information alone is not enough. The problem is not lack of information. We need something to seize our insides and galvanize us. You can always tell when a vision is beginning to be birthed. You will lose sleep over it. You will find yourself being defensive about it, almost as if you own it! You may even weep over it. You will find confusions and contradictions in the poor arguments against it.

For instance, someone mentioned that immigrants have come to benefit from life in the United States, so they are more open to the gospel here. We also have preachers on radio and television all day long, year-round, so the gospel is available to them. Yet as I looked into this "unreached" group, I found these leaders were often more committed in their ways to the old view of life. They wanted the economic benefits of the new environment without the religious baggage that they often see as simply part of the wider culture. Indeed, I found many of them—especially first-generation immigrants—to be more committed to the religions of their birth lands than had they stayed in their homelands. Since a part of their identity was found in their religious worldview and national heritage, they didn't want to give those up for mere economic benefit. Here they were, with no good grasp of the gospel, giving little attention to White or Black preachers—the color of traditional ministry leaders in the United States. Yet they maintained regular contact with the majority culture in the context of their vocation. They had the gospel available, but availability and accessibility are worlds apart when it comes to people from a different value and worldview systems. What could I do for this group? I was one of them.

Again, "When [Jesus] saw the multitudes, he was *moved* with compassion" (Matt. 9:36 NKJV, italic added). If you paraphrase that verse, it reads, "Jesus experienced a gut reaction that affected Him physically." The butterflies in Jesus' stomach stopped flying in formation. His compassion evoked an emotional response to the need.

Personal Responsibility: The fourth stage of progress in balancing information and emotion in moving from needs to opportunities can be described as a gradual shaping of an increasing sense of personal responsibility. The compassion that Jesus experienced, you can experience too. It is not primarily a feeling but a state in which emotion moves into conviction and action. Jesus took and commissioned personal responsibility for the needs He saw. He described the need, with Himself and His disciples included in the picture.

Let me identify several aspects that may come into play as we take personal responsibility for needs—our opportunities. These include divine openings, strategizing, and finding arenas to use your gifts.

DIVINE OPENINGS

Remember, unless you are sensitive to the environment and world around you, you will not be able to detect openings and discover occasions that increase your sensitivities to the world. "God has purposes and missions that are higher than any life mission I can conceive for myself. I believe God has a better use for my life than I could dream up on my own, so I surrender my life to His purpose for it."[2] And He brings them to pass, opens up opportunities and obstacles that you would not have envisioned in your outmost dreams.

For me, divine openings occurred in numerous ways, as I moved toward and "saw" the international business professional leader. On trips, I began exchanging business cards with topflight international leaders. They were ordinary human beings with the same human needs. Then friends began calling to ask if I had any materials that they could share with their employer or owner from another religious persuasion. "I'd like you to meet my VP of Planning; could you make some time? He comes from Brazil." Or "My company has just been bought out by an international group. They have asked me to serve as president for three years. I want to use it as an opportunity for the gospel among internationals. Do you have anything I can share with them?" Next, we had immigrant and international "converts" from these other religions asking us for material. What did I have that I could give to them? Some lengthy talks, book-length stuff, but these business professionals were like the rest. They wanted short introductions to every possible subject. Finally, I came across a number of fine Christian businesspeople traveling overseas, who wanted to bear witness to their overseas counterparts by leaving something for them. There were crying needs everywhere.

Jesus emotes in Matthew 9 that the multitudes were like sheep without a shepherd. To me, that description conveyed not only the needy status of the multitudes but Jesus' deep feeling for them. How long would I be dull of hearing? A dunce with a hardened heart? Divine openings connected with the realm of my gifts, my brokenness, and my resources prompt me to do something to impact this new immigrant group—the only identifiably unreached group in America.

ACTIVE STRATEGIZING

The Lord's strategy to meet the need of the crowds was to ask His disciples to pray and then send them out (cf. Luke 10:2–3). Here is the sequence: *First pray, and then do something about it.* So I found myself actively strategizing to meet the needs of these international leaders.

The mayor of Suva in Fiji received four tapes and played them for anyone who dared to ride with him across the main island to a golf course. "We don't have time for long sermons, but short ones are very useful." Aha! There came the opportunity. Could we turn our ministry radio messages into an audio-tract format, as a pass along tape or CD, for free distribution? Yes, said everyone from the producer to our office personnel. Many other questions arose. How would we qualify the business professional? By their knowledge of English and access to e-mail. How often? Monthly, for twelve months, like a free copy of the *Reader's Digest*. The format? Same as radio, on a high-energy music bed except with a different "intro" and "outro." What is our delivery system? We are in process of shaping this aspect.

Needs consistently turn into opportunities. Not all needs are opportunities, but opportunities are found within the needs. The dominant opportunities become the way to adopt strategic burdens for your life.

As you saw above in the case of our international leaders' ministry, we went through a "narrowing" process, putting needs through a filter that connected with my limited resources and experiences in one area of ministry. We narrowed it down thus: U.S. internationals, to new immigrants, to immigrant and international leaders, to the English-speaking and technologically literate among them. My resources were in English, and I found a "genetic fit" between what we did for English-speaking opinion leaders in Asia and Africa with what we could offer to this narrow group. It is now an issue of finding the right delivery system for the limited resources we could offer the group.

So you won't be simply seduced by needs, since a need is not a call in itself, stay the course in processing the present here and now. If you don't operate from scar-based ministry, you will have to pursue a need-based ministry or support those ministries with "time, talent, and treasure." You will have a dimension of divine direction too. Align your giftedness with needs and see if you can do anything with it—but make it the means to the mission. Align brokenness and needs and make it your opportunity, an additional mission toward the fourth segment of your life. See where you can connect gifts and brokenness and you will be a powerful person for God's Vision.

FROM NEEDS
AND OPPORTUNITIES TO ARENAS

As you identify your opportunities, those opportunities identify specific arenas in which to use your gifts. Arenas of service are the areas that provide the context for the exercise of your gifts toward God's big Vision. You can find arenas in which to minister from either the scars in your heart, or from the availability of your spiritual gifts in meeting specific human needs. For instance, I may want to exercise my gift of helps, but it will probably be in a different arena of impact than my wife, who is loaded with "helps." Arenas are narrower than opportunities and are critical to the placement of gifts. Gifts were not given so much to limit you, but their inherent limitations allow you to narrow your service. Beware! Unused gifts get rusty. Get with it. Now!

Gift and arena overlap in God's side of the process of fulfilling your vision. If gift enables you to find your vision, arena helps you identify the *place* of service. Just like you surveyed the opportunities that God has opened up for your gifting, you look at the arenas God has opened for the use of your gift.

For instance, God has not opened up ongoing children's ministries for me. I suppose if I wanted to, I could make myself speak to kids. Occasionally, I speak at a high school graduation, but I haven't done elementary school exercises. I once spoke to a group of senior citizens at a sunny Florida camp and knew that wasn't to be my present arena. I challenged them on commitment to Christ. Instead, they preferred to discuss winter weather up North. I would preach my heart out, only to see them head out on their golf carts to play shuffleboard within a few minutes of having heard another challenging message to serve Christ! This was not my arena.

On the human side of arena building, send feelers out for new arenas of service, so you can challenge your self-complacency. As a matter of increasing faith, test out the waters in new arenas in case God wants you to expand to new areas of ministry. Your gift often develops and surprises you in challenging situations. If you are young in your faith in Christ, try your hand in a wide variety of arenas, within and outside your giftedness, inside and outside comfort zones. You will foster growth, make discoveries, and even experience the blessing of ministry satisfaction.

Arenas of ministry often have to do with your interests in God's work. Where do you think you can make your best contribution toward God's vision? Or better stated, *Where do you think God can best use your life?* Where do you think you can really make a difference in people coming to God? Or better, *Where can God use you to bring people to Himself?* Just as you studied your Star-Scar Sketch to detect sensitivities, and as you consider your gifts to discover opportunities, think also about the context of those ministry accomplishments. Where have you seen your gifts being used best? With a certain group of people? In a particular kind of way? Then trust the Lord to open up similar arenas for your ministry utility.

I leave you, then, with two questions you can use in finding the arena for your gifts:

1. *What audiences receive best from you?* Men, women, senior citizens, junior highers, international students, widows, etc.?

2. *Where can Jesus use me to make a real difference in these lives?* Not necessarily a unique difference, though that uniqueness is an important ingredient in defining your arena. If God has opened up scarcer,

smaller, narrower arenas for impact, concentrate on them. (Dale works with sailboat racers, David with European non-Christian businessmen, Dwight with Asian Christian businessmen, Deepak with IT professionals, Don with antique restorers, Debbie with doctors, etc.)

I am terribly grateful for the wide number of arenas that could be opened up for my service. I can't simply go by my comfort zones or audiences in this matter. Consequently, I ask the second question emphasizing impact and profitability. Not comfort, not results, but utility and impact. In what arena can God use, invest, spend my gifts to profit Himself best and please Himself most?

This morning I talked with a man in transition. Fifty-five years of age, he knows his gifting, temperament, talents, and seasons. I asked him to work through the arena of his next step. He made a beginning as he acknowledged that God has placed American pastors and their personal, spiritual lives on his heart. Would this be the probable arena of his vision under the Vision? Will this be the best arena to make a difference, have an impact, do some profitable things for the Lord in the next season of his life? He alone must answer this question before God.

When you go from needs to opportunities and from opportunities to arenas, you can optimize life for God. You will gain personal direction for the Vision. You can extend and expend your gifts toward your vision. Let's face it. There are too many needs around us. Even the hardest hearts among us are occasionally drawn to human needs.

How can you exhibit more than a passing flight of sympathy that you display during the evening news? By processing your past and present. In this way, you can keep from the seductions of geographical closeness and imitate the God who doesn't succumb to spatial determinants of human need. Bear in mind also that you can only optimize your life for God. Maximizing your life, becoming significant, or "fulfilling your potential" is left to God's prerogatives and placements in your ongoing surrender to Him. These are God's roles.

Pursuing Personal Vision

Handwritten margin notes:
Sis. Jonzell
Put our plan on the back burner
Our plans, etc (dung)
Faith-we K in His hands
A vision w/o CAPACITY is only desire

Jigs, my friend's free-running dog, was rear-ended by a speeding car. His broken hind legs healed up . . . wrong. Now, when he breaks out running, those two dangling hind legs eventually end up in front of his good legs. Instinctively, Jigs does a U-turn to compensate thus making no perceivable progress.

If we live in the past, particularly our brokenness, we will make no advance. We cannot live backward. If we revisit scars, open up wounds, and wallow in the "unfairness of it all," we allow those experiences to keep us imprisoned in the past. The Intentional Life doesn't suppress scars but translates that information into understanding and direction. Intentional living means not giving power to the past to keep us in confinement. We understand life backward, but we do not live there.

> *Is there anything worse than not having your sight? Oh yes, it would be much worse to have your sight, but not to have vision.*
> ❧ HELEN KELLER

Neither can we live in the future. Tomorrow has not yet come. It is best to leave tomorrow's anxieties for tomorrow. Each day has enough troubles of its own (Matt. 6:34). We

Handwritten: Strategy - Capacity - Action

refuse to live in the past; we cannot live in the future. We live *in,* but not *for,* the present. We live *for,* but not *in,* the future.

How do we go about thinking about a "personal vision" for the future? We have sketched the past to reveal our sensitivities, studied the present to obtain opportunities, and now we will put together a personal vision for the future under God's Vision. May I suggest some policies and practices?

> ➢ Alongside the three segments/dimensions of personal life, family, and work, also affirm a ministry segment.

> ➢ Consider your epitaph.

> ➢ Prioritize your opportunities and responsibilities.

A FOURTH DIMENSION—MINISTRY

Here you go beyond renovation of your life to reorientation, processing each part of your mission—personal, family, and work—through, under, and around God's Vision and intentionally adding a fourth dimension—ministry. This fourth segment is not so much an addition as an orientation, an affirmation, and a solution. Since you want to go beyond occasional, passive forays into God's Vision and want to live life energized and propelled by God's Vision, this fourth segment is critical to enriching your other segments. If before you were even saved, God has prepared good works for you to fulfill (Eph. 2:8–10), you had better engage in ministry. An important part of the reason that you are a follower of Jesus today is because one or more other believers added "ministry" to their life missions. They went beyond personal, family, and work considerations to the fourth dimension of fulfilling their ministry. As a result, God's good news reached you. In what ways have you passed it on?

We divide ministry life into two areas: ministry to believers and unbelievers—to the church and to the world. Ask yourself two questions:

1. How is Jesus going to use my life to serve the church?
2. How is Jesus going to use my life in reaching the world?

Jesus' church includes the local church and the global church. What is your contribution to the local church family to which you belong? One of the elders of our church, a cardiologist by vocation, spends a great amount of time employing his gifts of wisdom and teaching at the church. His vocation provides the resources to fulfill his mission in life, family, work, and ministry. His vocation becomes a means to an end.

You also belong to the global church family—beginning with any Christian outside your church and extending to Christians throughout the world. You could pursue a vision along with churches in your immediate neighborhood—as specific as rallying for laws against pornographic intruders, and even recruiting non-Christians in this moral enterprise. Or you could volunteer time to help parachurch organizations. Here you adopt them as part of your vision for the world because their vision compels your heart. In this way, two visions coalesce to accomplish God's Vision for the world.

The other part of your ministry life relates to the world. The world comprises pre-Christians, both near and far. We shouldn't be exclusively involved with Christians if God's Vision is to bring glory to Himself among those who have not yet trusted Him. I encourage you in your journey toward maturity to intentionally take forays into discomfort. Cross the racial, cultural, or linguistic divides that are built into your company, community, city, and country. Consider even crossing national boundaries into an adventure into the unknown and unfamiliar parts of the world. How is God going to soften your heart, heighten your commitment, and enlighten your eyes unless you are willing to venture out for Him among nonbelievers? One of the reasons Christians from traditionally non-Christian majorities are prone to reach out to nonbelievers is because they have moved beyond peripheral awareness to gut-level response. They actively strategize to reach them. This also explains why Christians in a community share the same vision—peripheral awareness turns into strategy and action.

Outside Bombay lives a couple whose special audience in God's Vision includes temple prostitutes. They befriend these young women who are captive in temple service, rescue them from sexual and ritual bondage, protect them from violent repercussions, and introduce them to a completely new identity and life. That's working God's Vision into a life mission.

Nita lives in Belaya Tserkov, Ukraine. She first went there with a team to teach a training course in moral values (using the life of Jesus) for teachers. Then school laws changed, barring access to those teachers. The rest of the team returned to the United States, but Nita stayed. During those brief months of investigating God's will for her life in Ukraine, Nita felt a great compassion for the orphans, the poor, and the needy of the city. With a crumbling currency complicated by hyper-inflation, ordinary citizens wished for former Communist days. To give them hope, Nita called upon a few women of California to join her in a "Heart to Heart" ministry. She lives alone in a forlorn apartment in Belaya Tserkov. Her first Thanksgiving and Christmas were especially hard on her in terms of homesickness, so she has foregone her summer visit home and instead planned a Thanksgiving-Christmas home assignment to cast vision, raise funds, collect clothes, and bring hope in the name of Jesus to Ukrainian outcasts. Her service has overtaken her vocation.

Certainly not everyone should move into full-time Christian vocation, but all of us should be open to it as part of belonging to God's program. Whatever your decision, you must become fully aware and participate in God's global Vision. Can you imagine what would happen if a large number of Christians worldwide began to see their lives as an offering to God for accomplishing His Vision?

CONSIDERING YOUR EPITAPH

In the Middle Ages certain monks kept human skulls in their rooms with the Latin inscription, *memento mori,* meaning "remember your death." Epitaph writing echoes Christian and Buddhist sentiment on life's brevity.

Instead of plying the crowded north-south Central Expressway in Dallas to work each day, I often take its eastern parallel, Greenville Avenue. As I turn south, I come across some of the finest lawns in all of Dallas, the grounds of the Restland Cemetery. Since I will go the way of all flesh, a place like that will welcome my carcass one of these days. The graveyard not only forces me to contemplate my mortality but also my priorities.

Leaders ask you to consider your eulogies—what you would desire to be said by those closest to you at your funeral.

Perhaps you feel it's too soon—you have too much you still need to do before you consider your eulogy. It may be well worth it for you to read Isaiah 38 to see how King Hezekiah grappled with that tension as he contemplated the predicted end of his days.

Like many storyboarding and compression planning

techniques, eulogy writing helps you plan backward, starting with your deathbed. As you contemplate your desired eulogy, you find out what is most important to you. Your wistful eulogy will enable you to understand your real drives in life. Your wishful thinking can be changed to willful practice. You begin to see what smothers you in daily life, and then you can restructure life according to how you desire to be remembered. For example, yesterday I played touch football with my teenage kids, a nephew, and a neighbor. While my body is sore today, my spirit soars. I would like my kids to remember me as one who played ball on a beautiful fall day with them, rather than simply as a dad who let them play outside. Predeath reflection on your eulogy shows your true desires and harnesses your energies toward those priorities.

However, epitaph (rather than eulogy) writing would refer to daily mission—"he was a great dad and husband" or to ministry vision—"he modeled Christ to me." If my dad precedes me in death, we will eulogize him as a caring father, a faithful husband, and a hard worker. But those qualities do not reveal his personal vision and the unique role that he played in God's economy. Further, many non-Christians will fit the character of good fathers, moral husbands, and dedicated workers. In epitaph writing, you reflect your congruence with God's Vision to bring people to Himself, the difference God made through your life, and your personal contribution to that Vision. Those issues make you stand out as a *Christian* in this world. My father, at eighty, still uses his God-given gifts of wisdom, encouragement, and peacemaking to lead Christian leaders in jointly fulfilling God's Vision for their countries. Those who eulogize him will add the fourth dimension into their talks and thus virtually construct an epitaph for his tombstone.

Your epitaph could also reflect your missions in life. Have you heard of the "tombstone test"? If you had only six months to live, ask yourself: "What would you start doing that you haven't done?" and "What would you stop doing?" If you said you'd start spending more time with your family, start doing it now. This tombstone test would apply to anyone, Christian or non-Christian, and focuses your missions in personal, family, and work life.

Yet, I ask you as one named after and who follows the Savior of the world: "What should you start doing for Him that you haven't been doing?" In the fourth dimension of your mission, is your vision adjusting, aligning, and arising from His Vision? If you were to start doing ministry for Him, what would it say on your epitaph in relation to your vision and mission, your critical tasks, your ultimate perspectives with daily life?

To help you think this through, finish these two sentences about yourself:

He/she made God look great (mission) by

_____.

He/she made Jesus well known by

_____.

Don't make your epitaph too long or it won't fit on your gravestone. Also, don't think of it as "the law of the Medes and Persians that cannot be rewritten." Everything is provisional. That's why James asks us to include "if the Lord wills" on any future assertion (James 4:15). Remember, this is your present perception of the future, so it is not written in concrete. It can be changed by God's initiative. There will also be seasons when daily missions must be rebalanced and realigned, like car tires that pull your steering wheel one way.

You need to check the tires, get a wheel alignment, rotate them, or balance them so the car can keep running well. You want to discern when God is asking you to check unbalanced tires and when He is asking for shifts in destination. While submissively and significantly open to His changes, your epitaph reflects present reality in your self-discovery and self-definition process of identity, mission, and vision.

Think then, about your personal epitaph, reflect on God's work in your life, focus your mission, and then reorient all your existence to that vision under His Vision.

PRIORITIZING OPPORTUNITIES AND RESPONSIBILITIES

We all carry responsibilities in the daily, repeated segments of our lives. As we process these under our vision, I want you to clarify your mission in relation to vision. I can offer you three questions to help process and prioritize your personal mission under God's overall Vision.

The three "can and should" questions relate to the human doings of human beings—where and how can Jesus help Himself to my life? Can (ability/capacity) and should (motivation/obligation) function in tension. Work on specificity in each answer, because you are narrowing, focusing, and pointing to your unique contribution to God's harvest.

1. What does my life (my history, geography, seasons, gifts, etc.) specifically tell me about what I *can* and *should* do for the Lord Jesus Christ at this time?

2. What specific Christian needs *can* and *should* I do something about?

3. What specific non-Christian needs *can* and *should* I do something about?

The first question helps you clarify your vision. Where are you going? What do you want to change and contribute—the desired future effect of your life? What do you want to give and leave this world? If you don't know where you are going, you will not be grabbed, grasped, and galvanized by a vision. This is why many fine believers are *intensely* involved in life, without being *intentionally* involved in it. "Intensity" and "intention" come from the same root word, but the former persists in the present and the latter persists in the present with a view to the future. You can have your missional identity clear, but unless your visional destination is clarified, you are already shelved in the lost-baggage department of a busy airport.

As I study my life with its Stars and Scars, they all point to a global proclamation ministry in keeping with God's universal Vision to bring people to the Savior. I encourage you to find a simple two- or three-word phrase to describe your vision as a means to focus your life. I once asked leaders of nearly a hundred organizations at a banquet to reduce their work to one word. Ours was "proclamation." Every one of them struggled for that one word and then went on into elaborate explanations of that one word with many words! That short ministry word or phrase becomes the theme, the vision for your life.

Rick, an engineer, committed adultery in the twenty-second year of his marriage. How his marriage survived is an unexplainable but repeated picture of God's grace in enabling repentance and marital repair. His wife would acknowledge the disappointment, anger, and the shame that goes with her husband's philandering but said she vowed to be faithful to her covenant for better or worse. Rick was crushed enough to receive a new vision for his life. He now heads the men's fellowship in his church, fostering over thirty accountability groups. His key vision and ministry theme would be "men's accountability." The benefits of that vision are numerous, affecting the quality of families for a lifetime.

The second "can and should" question above—What Christian needs can and should I meet?—will evoke a list of needs around you, as well as what you can bring to finding and fulfilling your vision under the Vision.

My specific role regarding Christian needs has to do with strengthening pastoral leaders of weaker economies. There are many Christian needs around me. I will attend a funeral today of a forty-year-old man I hardly knew. His wife told me that he had wished for me to have a role in his funeral service. It will take seven hours of travel to be there for this family. However, notice that I am carrying on a *proclamation* ministry by speaking at this funeral. What if I chose not to speak at the funeral? I would then subsume my vision under my values. Since my values derive from Scripture, which encourages compassion and meekness (you may want to consult my early considerations of the Beatitudes and the Sermon on Mount as personal core values in Book One, *Soul Passion*), I would still consider being at this funeral for the sake of this young family. When values and vision coincide, there is no question; when they conflict, values take over vision. If we live a fraction of our time marching to the beat of a ministry vision, we will still bring profit to the Master.

Finally, let's look at the third question: What should we do for non-Christian needs? I point you to look next door. How can you minister to an unbelieving neighbor's needs in the area of your gifts and resources? Evangelism, Christian missions, compassion toward the hungry, homeless, and abused, etc. What specific non-Christian needs in your community, city, country, and worldwide can you and should you do something about?

While browsing through his newspaper, an interesting statistic caught Steve's eye. He saw that in 90 percent of divorce cases filed in his county, one of the partners wanted to save the marriage. That figure stuck in his conscience and heart. He decided to do something about it. He talked to his pastor, who talked to other pastors, and out of that formed an alliance of churches to offer a seminar to recently filed divorce cases, entitled, "How to Save Your Marriage Alone." They mailed notices of the seminar to those addresses. An incredible vision ignited the community for the sake of their people. Sixty percent of those who attended the seminar were able to save the marriages—alone! And many of them came to salvation.

What I do for non-Christian needs flows from how the Lord has worked in my life. I attempt to expose large numbers of non-Christian opinion leaders of weaker economies to the gospel. Again, these are primarily oriented toward proclamation gifts that God has entrusted to me at present.

Pak Chris leads the Evangelical Theological Seminary in Djodjakarta, Indonesia. You cannot be with him for more than five minutes and he is already exuding his vision for his great land. "Vision Indonesia One, One, One"—one church, in one village, in one generation. He is getting increasingly recognizable by both believers and nonbelievers in that country. Since the land has quaked economically and religiously, I thought I would test him out with a fair question. I asked if he should consider heading a political party and run for the presidency of his country? Immediately he replied that his vision for Indonesia wouldn't be accomplished by his turning into a political leader. He wants churches planted all across his land so that the majority would hear the gospel, receive Jesus, and be incorporated into the church. In the first twenty years of his vision (1975–1995; he is gunning for June 30, 2015 as finale), the number of churches in Indonesia has doubled, primarily by his students: they must plant a church as a graduation requirement. You, too, can live by and march to the beat of a personal vision under the grand Vision of bringing people to God.

So add "personal vision—ministry" to your missions in life as your fourth segment. Christians who understand God's large Vision and proceed to finding personal vision will still feel that they are buildings turned backward unless they add personal vision to their personal mission. I was once driving an associate to the airport and decided to take a side street because the main road was jammed. Unfamiliar with the side streets but having an idea of where I was, I kept proceeding. He said, "I am all turned around." I replied, "I, too, am all turned around." The only difference: I knew where I was, but he didn't, even though we both knew our destination. Knowing where I was and where I was going really helped in the middle of the present confusion. In the same way, when personal vision informs and directs your daily mission, it will help you keep going in the middle of confusion, imbalance, and jammed traffic.

Making your personal vision the fourth dimension of personal mission, turning your vision into a regular dimension of life, requires changes. But in the process, you'll live the Intentional Life for God as well. That addition will significantly help in the middle of confusion. Self-understanding is not enough. You have to apply that understanding to reality. Don't engage in self-understanding without engaging in changes. The ministry life becomes the lead dog, the tow truck, and the railway engine in your life. The rest of life aligns to its drawing power.

Just as you set goals for your life missions, a TARGET of goals to plan and implement, you also want to pursue objectives and initiatives consistent with your vision. Take those latter two questions—the specific Christian needs and non-Christian needs that you "can and should" meet. Create two columns and write down as many as you can identify. When you finally start repeating yourself, you've come to the end of your present awareness. Group them in categories, perhaps by location or kinds of needs, such as "needs at my church" or "physical needs" that you can and should meet. Don't write what you think should be done without accompanying limits of your ability. Vision is harder and more definite than mere wishing or dreaming. Of course, the more the ability, the more the responsibility. Group them into three or four areas and they will turn into your "vision plan."

Here I add the distinctly Christian component of faith to find and fulfill your vision. Faith is not presumption nor prediction but an active yielding to almighty God in anticipation for what He will do through your abandonment to Him. Since whatever is not of faith is sin, you cannot hold a vision about which you do not sense increasing conviction. Also, your faith may be clear as to the ends but not as to the means. Broadly speaking, "faith" in the Bible is *instrumental* when it comes to salvation but seems to be an *endowment* when it comes to prayer requests or service. If you can't continue to pray about a delayed answer with increasing conviction, stop praying for it. Leave the matter with the Holy Spirit, who can interpret your desires to the Father. Similarly, ask God to increase your conviction about a ministry vision. Raise your sights in faith. Are you ever bold for God? Pull the trigger. Be ambitious for God, but let it be *godly* ambition. Godly ambition differs from selfish ambition. When you are not competing, envying, or mimicking peers, and are willing to subject your vision to an accountability group, your ambition toward the Vision is more godly than selfish.

To summarize these chapters on developing a personal vision into a life mission, we have dealt with the launch of the Intentional Life toward God's Vision. The basic spiritual impulses to understanding personal vision will be:

> ➤ Scar based via experiential sensitivity to narrow your focus (2 Cor. 1:3–7);

> ➤ Gift based through endowed inclination to identify your roles (1 Cor. 12:7);

> ➤ Need based using external opportunity to call on your resources (Matt. 9:36–38); and

> ➤ Debt based by growing internal conviction to prompt your intentional engagement (Rom. 1:14).

This final factor, the obligatory burden, requires comment and development.

FROM NEEDS, OPPORTUNITIES, AND ARENAS TO BURDENS

While just one of these four areas can drive your personal vision, the more they overlap, the clearer you will be as to your unique participation in God's Vision—your strategic "burden(s)." In the mix of the four bases, you have moved from needs to opportunities to arenas to burdens. Below I note supplemental components of implementing an effective, intentional, burden: strategy, capacity, and action.

Strategy
Vision without strategy is mere desire. When you strategize

to accomplish your vision, you carry a *strategic* burden. If you spend any time at all "visioning" or growing your burden, you will notice that you are always thinking of ways to accomplish that vision. After identifying core mission areas for personal, family, work, and ministry life and prioritizing them, write out a strategy for each of those visionary areas toward your ministry vision. "Strategy is one's commitment to a vision of the future." "Strategy is fundamentally about identifying and pursuing opportunity." Strategy "refers to moving an enterprise forward in a planned and coordinated way."[1] What are you going to do about the vision in your life missions? How are you going to accomplish ministry opportunities in and from those platforms?

When the evangelistic needs of opinion leaders began to turn into personal opportunities for ministry enough to become my personal vision, I sensed that an advanced secular degree would give me the platform to address these groups. It is not unusual for me to simply be introduced as "a spiritual philosopher with an advanced degree in philosophy from the University of Delhi, India" to provide a credible platform for addressing spiritual issues in the lives of my audience. Otherwise I'd just be another Christian preacher giving an opinion to these leaders. Since I have tasted their side of worldviews, these opinion leaders give me the privilege of articulating my message with a semblance of attention. Getting an advanced degree was a strategy in the pursuit of a vision. That strategy has been accomplished and new ones to reach these audiences have emerged. Strategies need to be flexible. You may add or subtract from them.

Capacity
God gives visions to *individuals*. Take that vision to counselors (a formal or informal board) who will help you with

articulating and evaluating strategy to pursue that vision. Then trust the Lord to provide you the capacity to implement the strategy to accomplish your visionary burden.

Capacity includes the resources you have specified above. Remember that capacity begins in your spiritual life. From your passion for Christ comes internal energy to think, communicate, and recruit for your vision. If your spiritual life is not in order, consider time off for replenishment. Work through the disciplines we have mentioned under passion (see *Soul Passion*—Book One). Include your spouse and children in vision sharing, strategic planning, and capacity building. Think about how your vocation contributes to the vision. Occasionally I hear men say, "My vision is to introduce children to Christ; my profession (lawyer, engineer, doctor, etc.) pays the bills." Their profession becomes part of the capacity needed to fulfill the vision.

Some time ago a local businessman came to me with a vision to disseminate Christian truth to the public by building a theme park with a full-sized Noah's ark as his strategy. A biblical vision and an attractive strategy indeed. He wanted to locate it around the largest outlet mall in the world (remember we live in Texas with the largest *everything* in the world). I endorsed his vision and enjoyed hearing about his strategy, but I couldn't encourage him immediately because he simply didn't have the capacity to pull it off. Other business leaders have dissuaded him for the same reason. I haven't given up on his desire (a vision without strategy and capacity is only desire), but I suggested he come up with a "capacity" plan before people will take him seriously.

Building capacity enables strategies to be turned into action and marks intensity with intentionality. But don't do it in the way of the Mexico City government in the late 1970s. I read of how they increased the capacity of the *Viaducto,* a four-lane motorway, by repainting lines to make it six lanes wide—in effect, a 50 percent increase in capacity. Unfortunately, this also resulted in an increase in fatal accidents. After a year, the *Viaducto* was changed back to a four-lane road—a 33 percent capacity reduction. The government, casting around for facts to support its claims for social progress, subtracted that 33 percent reduction from the 50 percent increase to claim a net increase in capacity of 17 percent.[2]

Action

"The vision must be followed by venture," said the late Vance Havner. "It is not enough to stare up the stairs. . . . We must step up the stairs." Your action plans (or *tactical* plans) will follow the TARGET model from our previous treatment on personal mission. Action plans detail and apply strategies to accomplish your objectives or goals.

Back to my strategy of an advanced secular degree to reach the international leaders, the goal in my action plan was to finish the degree. The plan called for me to finish it much earlier than I eventually did. Since goals are adjustable (see TARGET of Goals in *Soul Mission*), I did not give up even though I faced administrative boondoggles at the university and pressing life demands in family and ministry seasons. That strategy was finally accomplished and the goal achieved.

Since vision is being transferred into mission, you must implement action plans in ministry life even as you pursue action steps in personal, family, and work life. Ministry life becomes today's mission when you go on from need to burden to strategy to capacity to ACTION. Now your "todays" begin to count for repeated pleasure to the Master as you carry your ministry burden into daily mission. Tomorrow's vision will be a part of tomorrow's mission, so you want to be careful with how you prepare for the glory of God tomorrow today—by strategic thinking, capacity building, and action planning.

Trust the Lord with your personal vision for His ministry and you will be amazed as to how He gets through to you, shapes you, focuses it, and accomplishes His plans for the planet through you. Remember, you have discovered His Vision for you and are submitting to it. God honors your submission with a specific role in compelling vision for impacting people anywhere.

I mentioned earlier that one of my two strategic burdens is to provide skills and tools for pastoral leaders in weaker economies. God provided a personal past to launch that vision. The personal present confirms that vision. In 1993, I headed into a September board meeting of *RREACH* International with the strategy of an international pastors conference to rally a core group of key pastoral leaders as owners and distributors of the vision. All I knew was the date—2001—the beginning of a new millennium. The next May, as we entered into a high-powered planning meeting at Dallas Theological Seminary, I received a caution. Someone using the room in a previous meeting had written out a verse on the whiteboard, "Do you seek great things for yourself? Do not seek them" (Jer. 45:5 NKJV). I was really open to the Lord's guidance on this matter. I checked my motives and quietly prayed: "Lord, I don't think I am seeking great things for myself. But if I am, please stop this process. Only You know my heart."

The next months were filled with prayer for direction and wisdom. I didn't want to default in the role that God had given me. On the other hand, I didn't want to pursue what might not be God's will through me for His world. Three weeks prior to the next board meeting, I attended a faculty retreat. I fell on my knees and opened my Bible for direction. It fell open to Jeremiah 45 and my eyes fell on verse 5. "But you, are you seeking great things for yourself? Do not seek them" (NASB). I said to myself, "That's it!" That strategy was over. I did not take it to our governing board. The Lord honored that decision and opened up another far more effective way of accomplishing the same vision.

As a pastoral training ministry, we get to provide skills and tools to thousands of pastoral leaders each year. That's a large number, but there are two million of them in Asia, Africa, Latin America, and the former USSR, of whom only 5 percent possess formal education. I decided to write to a dozen organizations about meeting together to discuss the immense opportunity represented by 1.9 million pastoral leaders without training. The Billy Graham organization said they wanted to cosponsor the event. They generously offered their Wheaton College facilities and expanded the scope. In March 1997, I was at a Promise Keepers speakers' summit and shared the vision with Bruce Wilkinson. In typical "Prayer of Jabez" fashion, he remarked, "This is a huge vision, Ramesh. How many are you expecting at the event?" I said, "We are inviting fifty and think that twenty-five will be there." He affirmed me and said, "Trust the Lord to bring all fifty CEOs to the event." Something remarkable happened. We had to close registrations. Ninety-nine organizations were represented. A special mantle of leadership was endowed on me for those two days of fellowship and partnership. We don't know how God is going to take this vision and strategy, but we are open, humble, and available. An entirely new organization has been launched for strategizing, building capacity, and executing that vision.

I use this illustration humbly to remind us that God is in charge of vision and process, resources and favor, objectives and strategies. He runs His own agenda, makes His own timetable, and sets the stride. The question is whether we will lock into His Vision.

In fact, I suggest that you add another sheet of paper to your personal interaction with the recommended study tools in this Intentional Life trilogy. Having brainstormed all those suggestions, this new sheet of paper will bring a most defining moment to you. First, sign your name at the bottom with a pen. Then write out your present understanding of the strategic burden(s) you want to carry toward His Vision *in pencil*. If He so desires, let God change whatever He wants on that page. Don't, however, submit a blank page to God—that doesn't compliment His narrative and creativity in you. Give Him an erasable one, a word-processing folder or file that can be revised, rewritten, and resaved under your name.

Only God creates *ex nihilo*. You may come up with a hundred ideas at night or in the shower but keep in mind that it is God's Vision that you are about. He is not about your vision. When your vision coalesces with His, He unleashes opportunities and resources for you to accomplish His will. Hold your vision loosely. If you hold too tightly, you'll choke it; if you hold carelessly, you'll neglect it. Hold it loosely, depending on God to implement it in His way and time.

The Intentional Life—comprised of passion, mission, and vision takes you from where you are to where you should be so you don't have to wonder where you have been. God takes the initiative in this creative process, prompts you to consider the plans He has for you, and provides the resources for you to discern, understand, and implement His vision for you. Since His ways are higher than ours, His Vision for our lives will always be greater than we can conceive. God takes the small pieces of our life—its triumphs and tragedies—and turns them into a fulfillment of His Vision for the world if we surrender to finding and doing His will by His ways in our lives.

May I encourage you to read through these last three chapters a second and third time slowly, to apply the findings in your life? Hundreds of students have written thousands of pages in discovery, definition, and decision following the method shared in this work. I share the following letter of testimony to help motivate you to take the time, thought, and discipline to write out the objectives and action steps to process your life vision.

Dear Dr. Richard:

Thank you for the great admonishment and encouragement in your spiritual life class last semester. I especially appreciated the life-mapping project. As I mentioned, I was (am) in a time of transition in ministry. God used that paper as a great time or way for me to focus and define where He is leading me. It sharpened my vision and moved me to more confidently step out in new areas.

As a result, God has led me to resign from _____ (after twelve years) and apply to _____. I have seen His hand clearly in the process as I've continued to evaluate my spiritual gifts, passion, and vision for ministry goals. It has been an incredible process—to step out in faith! He is faithful indeed!

Thank you for challenging me to evaluate and focus more clearly on how God desires to use me to best serve Him! Thank you for your dedication to helping shape students like myself!

In Him,

C.B.

The exercise of focusing your vision under His Vision is not empty idealism forged out of mere theoretical considerations. It is realistic and will shape the rest of your Intentional Life.

Conclusion

"It has no plot, no climax, no denouement; no beginning, no middle and no end." That was one response to Samuel Beckett's famous play *Waiting for Godot* on opening day in London, 1955.[1] Long years ago that pronouncement would have been called a critique. These days it is safer to view the remark as a description. A description laced with sadness, disappointment, and frustration concerning a play that seemed to portray the real life of its author. One of his lovers called Beckett *Oblomov,* a byword in Russian literature for "inertia."[2]

> *Every day we ought to renew our purpose.*
>
> ⁊ THOMAS À KEMPIS

Your life is far from inertia, but have you acknowledged its lack of plot? No outline, no guiding principle, no controlling purpose. How would you like the crowning statement of your life to read: "He had no plot!"? Does that phrase sound like your present life?

Fortunately, human ingenuity manufactures small purposes to live for, even if it has no great purpose to live by. In Book One, *Soul Passion,* we began by saying that a low purpose life is certainly better than a no purpose life. But high purpose living is preferable to low purpose living. By design and desire, God calls us to an Intentional Life, to pursue the highest purpose for the best possible earthly life—His life purpose for you, lived by His life presence in you. Discerning, nurturing, implementing that highest purpose is the best way to enter, evaluate, exist, and enjoy your life.

Some Christians recognize a theology of purpose but then live randomly.

"I want to thank you," said a Native American, puzzling me with an unexpected overflow of gratitude at our first-time meeting. He went on, "I thank every person from India for my classification as an Indian. I'm glad Columbus was looking for India and not for Turkey!"

Columbus's way of exploration may characterize your life. "When he began, he didn't know where he was going; when he got there, he didn't know where he was; and when he returned, he didn't know where he had been! And all of it he did on other people's money! Several times in just one decade. For money!"[3]

Does your life approximate Columbus's life more than Oblomov? Are you preoccupied with keeping the ship afloat, not knowing where you are headed, or whether you are going or coming? I prepared and provided these thoughts and resources with every intention to help you live life advantageously and impactfully.

The most important ingredient in finding direction is position, even more than knowing destination. At the "Fur Trade and Exploration" (1741–1860) exhibit of the Royal B.C. Museum in Victoria, British Columbia, I read the following words on navigation: "Knowing one's position, direction, and speed is the essence of navigation. Of these, position is hardest to find, but once obtained, speed becomes obvious by measuring the time taken to move from one known point to another. As to direction, reliable compasses have been available since the thirteenth century."

Passion, what you love, reveals positional information. Passion functions as the positional foundation for your spiritual journey. For life building, I recommended a singular, spiritual priority among your passions. Ultimately, the underlying passion of your life must be the Lord Jesus Christ Himself.[4] Your relationship to Him gives you assurance, identity, and cohesion. Don't seek your identity in what you do. Find it in your unmerited relationship of total acceptance by God as His child, His love, and His delight. Much discouragement will arise if you ground your worth upon superior performance in the dimensions of life. You will make many mistakes, commit numerous sins, and foolishly carry an overload sure to invite discouragement. The revitalization of life will rise from your consistent, spiritual walk with the God who creates, leads, and sustains the journey. When love for Him is missing, everything in life becomes a job description. To keep your life from being mere duty, ground it in vibrant love of God.

Two Christmases ago, my brother's family planned a visit. My kids had not seen their cousins for a while and simply longed to be with them. While the adults were attempting to figure out activities for them (at least as a way to keep the decibel level down), my son remarked, "Don't worry, Dad, as long as we are going to be with our cousins, it doesn't matter if we have nothing to do!" He reflected the kind of satisfaction that we must derive from our relationship with Jesus. He alone would be enough. Everything else, mission and vision are bonuses! Let's not make our performance in mission and vision the source of our identity, joy, and fulfillment. If we do, we will be easy candidates for burnout and dejection.

Hospitalized with a heart attack and placed in an intensive care ward for several weeks before he returned to work, a colleague asked himself three questions: Can I be content with anonymity? Can I make it with just the Lord? Do I realize that I am not indispensable, that the ministry will go on without me? The middle question reflects the controlling aspect of a human being—that of loving the Lord Jesus Christ for who He is with all you've got.

Do you value Him above all else? To be a human being without human loving is impossible. But loving God distinguishes your humanness in the first place, restores you to the original grade, and fulfills the foremost commandment. You will find that underlying passion informs your undergirding purpose. God undergirds the one who makes Him the passion of life. You are positioned on Him, His love for you and your love for Him, even before you seek and travel to your destination.

"Human being" not only comprises human *loving* but also human *doing* and human *going*. Loving, doing, and going follow an ontological, psychological, logical, and even chronological order. The distinction between human being and mere animal existence arises from human beings engaging in purposeful existence—choosing their lovings, doings, and goings.

Human *doing* remains part of purposeful human *beings,* except your "doings" may simply be a repetition of the mundane while loving it. But as you do your doings, you will find your doings enable your goings.

On the foundation of a vital love for God, build a life that is spent for God's glory—the ulterior purpose for everything you must do—as a person, spouse, parent, child, employer, employee, entrepreneur, executive, professional, housewife.

Give weight to God's glory in the details of your life, and His glory will carry the weights you must carry in daily life. Make your fundamental *mission* the glory of God. In everything you do, whatever you do, wherever, whenever, however you do it, let Him be honored. In this way you can be a human being in your human doing. Unlike non-Christians, carnal and baby Christians, you will seek to make God look good in the repeated dimensions of life—personal, family, and work life.

Finally, human *being* requires human *going*. Unless we are going somewhere, we will end up nowhere, somewhere else, or anywhere. Where are you going in life? There are so many vital destinations and vibrant means, if you would only raise your sights to His Vision. You can go for God. This morning I read Jesus' words from John 15:16, "You did not choose me, but I chose you and appointed you *to go* and bear fruit." When you go for God, you bear earthly fruit, turn eternal profit, and make personal impact. After positioning yourself right, on God, go on to find His destination for life to pursue, to go after, under the compass of His Word, the captaincy of His presence, at the right speed.

One episode of the cartoon *Cathy* hits the nail on the head of superficial concerns in a comic sequence.[5] First frame: Cathy bemoans, "What a horrible dream! What a nightmare!!" In the second frame she asks, "What's wrong with me? A zillion problems in the world, and I'm thrashing around in my sleep, dreaming that I got a haircut! How superficial can you get? How petty and self-indulgent can one person be?" She goes on, "From this moment on, I vow to obsess only about the important, globally significant issues that affect the lives of all man and womankind." In the final frame she bawls, "I'm all out of fake sweetener for my coffee" as she fills her coffee cup.

If you have felt the superficiality, the frivolous focus of Cathy's life in your own, renew your membership in the human club. We love to go after culturally approved norms, the existentially immediate, the personally pleasurable issues of life. But Christianity is more than a dog chasing its tail, or humanity running any race it chooses. The "Christian" appellation—adjective or noun—calls for you to run His race, finish His course, implement His vision. So raise your sights, deepen your life, and place your weight down on right priorities. That differentiates you from carnal Christians and baby Christians.

The Intentional Life consists of passion, mission, and vision. Like other considerations in this trilogy, these three overlap and overlay each other in God and in you. Unless your vision is clear, passion depletes at the first obstacle, and life's missions get confused. If your passion is fragile, then missions become random, following an unknown or unclear vision. If mission fails, passion flounders, and you will pursue a fantasy tomorrow. However, a biblically prescribed purpose, made up of underlying passion, ulterior mission, and ultimate vision, will provide you the undergirding purpose of your life. It will prepare, provide, pull, and push you for the rest of your life. Think of that purpose as a mountain to climb. Your passion for climbing keeps you going in your daily mission toward an ultimate vision; your mission is built on passion and sets your sights on the vision; and your vision energizes passion and justifies mission. Just like the mountain will carry you even as you climb it, your undergirding purpose will carry you while you climb it.

What is the purpose of life? Loving God, honoring God, serving God: To make the Lord Jesus Christ your first love, to make Jesus Christ look great, and to make Christ well known.

What is your purpose in life? Consider filling in the blanks below:

The purpose of (your name and family)_____is

to love God (passion) by _____

to honor God (mission) by _____

to serve God (vision) by _____

There are no perfect or quick answers to those blanks. But there are good answers if you don't try to fill them in overnight. Start where you are today. The spiritual life is not complex, but it is demanding. It is not complicated, but like brushing teeth, needs to be consistent. Ask God the Holy Spirit, who is more enthusiastic about your spirituality and more intentional about your purpose than you are, to infuse you with His energy for loving God. Put some basic habits of holiness into practice. Reinforce that foundation, keep it maintained to prevent structural breakdown.

Also, find simple ways to make God look good in personal, family, and work life. Declare your mission to glorify God in these dimensions and bring them under submission to that overall mission. Your practice of life, built on spiritual values and virtues, are permeated with the mission of upholding Christ's reputation in all areas of life.

And then, develop a distinctive, unique ministry flowing out of God's Vision: to bring all people to Himself. Bring this Vision to the repeated status of mission as a fourth dimension of life in addition to personal, family, and work life, toward God's glory.

The following ditty compares the human soul to the animal kingdom while motivating internal, intentional restructure.

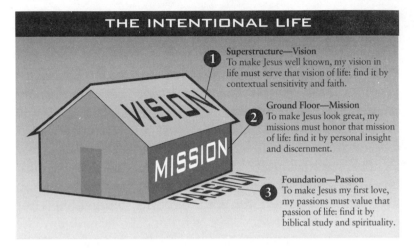

THE INTENTIONAL LIFE

1 Superstructure—Vision
To make Jesus well known, my vision in life must serve that vision of life: find it by contextual sensitivity and faith.

2 Ground Floor—Mission
To make Jesus look great, my missions must honor that mission of life: find it by personal insight and discernment.

3 Foundation—Passion
To make Jesus my first love, my passions must value that passion of life: find it by biblical study and spirituality.

My soul is like a barnyard duck
Muddling in the barnyard muck,
fat and lazy with useless wings.

But sometimes, when the north wind sings
And the wild ducks fly overhead,
it remembers something lost and dead.

It cocks a wary and bewildered eye
and makes a feeble attempt to fly.

Unfortunately it's fairly content with the state it's in,
but it's not the duck it might have been.[6]

From duck existence to human life, you need to recover what is lost and dead. The purpose of an Intentional Life is so you can be all you can be and not mourn what you might have been. It's not too late to start. Yes, you could have started decades ago, but the next best option is to begin immediately.

I want you to consider the rest of your life as an erased clean slate. You see the chalk residue of previous writings, but you have fresh chalk in your hand. The future is clean. The chalk is made up of the ingredients you have studied for clarifying mission and vision. You have received these as resources to steward, invest, and manage. You will now direct the rest of your life in light of the objectives you wrote out for yourself, family, work, and service. Only humans can rebuild life from scratch, again and again. If you qualify for the "human being" epithet, there is hope for your future. If you continue to mimic random animal life, you best resemble a beast of burden lumbering and slumbering through desert existence, a duck that might have been. To call yourself a human being would then be a euphemism. Instead, you can prevent the "human" title from becoming an exaggeration in describing you, by pursuing a spiritual journey toward a distinctive, unique, and intentional life.

Our biblical conviction recognizes that God doesn't make mistakes in our mistakes. It is sad that you have waited this long, but life is not wasted yet. Unlike buildings, humans don't have to build it right the very first time. Though a perfect building is preferable, we all sin, fail, and make mistakes. But everything is fixable by God, under God. You are in process, as I am. Even buildings are called "buildings," even though they should be called "built," if they already are. We are in process during the entirety of life until the day God presents us as finished testimonies to His workmanship. While in process, the intentional person pumps human intensity into discerning, nurturing, and implementing a life of intention.

In the final analysis you have two options:

1. You can spend the rest of your life waiting for death unintentionally, loving, doing, going about life in your own way. Check Longfellow's remorseful "Mezzo Cammin" and you sense this option:

Half my life is gone, and I have let
  The years slip from me and have not fulfilled
  The aspiration of my youth, to build
  Some tower of song with lofty parapet.

Not indolence, nor pleasure, nor the fret
  Of restless passions that would not be stilled,
  But sorrow, and a care that almost killed,
  Kept me from what I may accomplish yet.

Though half-way up the hill, I see the Past
  Lying beneath me with its sounds and sights,—
  A city in the twilight dim and vast,

With smoking roofs, soft bells, and gleaming lights,—
  And hear above me on the autumnal blast
  The cataract of Death far thundering from the
  heights.[7]

How does your life differ from a non-Christian's moaning and mourning?

Or

2. *You can spend the rest of your life intentionally.*

One of the greatest compliments I have received came from LaVerne—a mentor to me and my wife. Nobody I knew pursued the Intentional Life like her. Her prognosis after a mastectomy was "70 percent in two years and 90 percent in five." Somebody once remarked that the second hand on your watch goes "tick, tick, tick," until you get cancer, when it shouts "precious, precious, precious." In the third year, her blood tests revealed rapid escalation, and no one with blood tests like that had lived more than one year according to her oncologist. Deliberately and graciously (spiritual marks of the Intentional Life), LaVerne adopted the mission and vision of this book as her own—"to make God look good; and to make Christ well known"—and lived it better than I could. Listen to her telling intentionality:

I have an intense desire to finish my life strong by the grace of God. Not going from crisis to crisis but from strength to strength. I want to be an inspiration and a carrier of my faith. I pray the Lord will enlighten me to see His vision for my life, going boldly through every door He opens to me, embracing the gifts of wisdom, discernment, patience, discipline, endurance, love, and compassion. My life is a Divine Privilege.

Well beyond the days the oncologist had numbered for her, the Lord had numbered them differently. "I am ready to meet the Lord face to face, but until then I desire to live each as if I will go on forever. I am not focused on death but on life." She was fond of saying, "There is a Divine Privilege out there with your name on it. Tailor-made to your passions. I'd like to invite you to join me on the journey. Everything else pales in comparison to serving our Lord."

She celebrated her tenth anniversary since diagnosis with an evangelistic party for the entire medical community in her city! She found the Divine Privilege with her name written on it, the unique divine privilege under God's umbrella Vision, and turned it into personal mission.

A few months before she died, she decided to make God look great and Christ well known even at her funeral. She meticulously planned her final farewell. Her funeral day featured coordinated colors and arrangements of flowers; the "Hallelujah Chorus"; a silver baton with Isaiah 61:3 embossed for each of her grandkids; a letter written on private stationery to everyone who came to the memorial service. What a witness to the non-Christian civic and business leaders of a community, city, and church that she loved! Everyone knew Christ was her first love at that glorious event. We had to keep reminding ourselves that we were at a funeral. It was simply a farewell to one who lived this Intentional Life trilogy in life and death.

May I intentionally invite you to live the Intentional Life intentionally? You wouldn't think it would be easy to neglect life, would you? Your life is all around you and hangs around until your last breath. You may be immersed in life, burned out from it, and short of dying, live through it. It seems as if you'd take life more purposefully.

But you'd be surprised. Life's very busyness fosters randomness. Its complexity demands impulsiveness. Its unpredictability encourages arbitrariness. If you are preoccupied with maintaining life but not intentionally living it, God invites you to build an intentional, strategic, purposeful life comprised of:

> *A sturdy foundation for life*—God himself, our Soul's Passion. There is no limit to the edifice you'll build if the foundation of your life is a passionate relationship with God. Jesus called "loving God" the greatest of all the commandments. Make Him the foundation on which you live, the framework by which you live. You can have many passions *in* life but only one Passion *of* life. Make Jesus your first love.

> *A definitive floor plan and first floor to determine and decorate daily living*—everything in life for God's glory, our soul's mission. Your mission is to uphold His reputation. Your fundamental commitment is to make God look good in all of life's dimensions. You can have many missions *in* life pursuing personal, family, and work responsibilities but only one mis-

sion *of* life—to make Jesus look great in and out of those responsibilities.

➤ *A unique superstructure in implementing God's commission to bring salvation to all nations*—our soul's vision. His Vision galvanizes you into a distinctive service for Him. You may have many visions *in* life, but all must serve His Vision—the vision of your life—to make Jesus well known.

A friend hosted my family at his vacation home. He and I took our kids tubing, hauled behind a motorboat. Two toothless seven-year-olds made a pact to enjoy the ride together as board mates. We took the challenge and tried to knock these young ladies off the tube. We tried every plausible turn of the speedboat, sharp cuts, accelerated whips. The two clung on, hung on, stuck on. We couldn't shake them off. Finally the dads gave up on the game. When they knew that the dads had given up on shaking them loose, they let go of the rope.

Our next "passengers" were the girls again. We found them floating in the water with their tubes, giggling. They grabbed the towrope but released it as soon as we picked up speed and hit a few waves. The results were two tumbling kids splashing in the water. We had to repeatedly turn around and throw them the line to start over. Eventually, they swam to the boat, climbed up the ladder, dripping wet, tangled hair, and toothless grins.

"How come you let go of the rope?" I asked.

Our daughter exclaimed, "We did it on purpose! It was so fun to let go in the waves and tumble through the water!" We knew they clung on intentionally, but they had let go on purpose too.

One day, be it today or a long time from now, when we climb the staircase to heaven, I want each of us to be able say to any of the Lord's questions regarding our life, "We did it on purpose! We did life on purpose. We clung on to what should be held, on purpose. We let go of what wasn't needed in life, on purpose."

Go ahead and do life intentionally. Spend the rest of your life in loving, honoring, and serving God as your underlying, ulterior, and ultimate purpose in your unique way. Build an Intentional Life of passion, mission, and vision into a purposeful living structure to make the rest of your life worthy of your God, and worth it for yourself and others. Discern, nurture, and implement the Intentional Life.

Benediction

"This day I call heaven and earth as witnesses against you that I have set before you life and death, blessings and curses. Now **choose life,** so that you and your children may live and that you may love the LORD your God, listen to his voice, and hold fast to him. *For the LORD is your life.*"

> *Life is now in session.*
> *Are you present?*
>
> — B. COPELAND

—DEUTERONOMY 30:19–20

Endnotes

Chapter 1: Faulty Vision, Fuzzy Vision

1. *David:* "You have made my days a mere handbreadth; the span of my years is as nothing before you. Each man's life is but a breath. Man is a mere phantom as he goes to and fro: He bustles about, but only in vain" (Ps. 39:5–6).

2. *Jesus:* "Be on your guard against all kinds of greed; a man's life does not consist in the abundance of his possessions" (Luke 12:15).

3. *Samuel:* "The LORD does not look at the things man looks at. Man looks at the outward appearance, but the LORD looks at the heart" (1 Sam. 16:7).

4. *Daniel:* "He (God) changes times and seasons; he sets up kings and deposes them" (Dan. 2:21); or Isaiah. "He brings princes to naught and reduces the rulers of this world to nothing. No sooner are they planted, no sooner are they sown, no sooner do they take root in the ground, than he blows on them and they wither, and a whirlwind sweeps them away like chaff" (Isa. 40:23–24).

5. *Solomon:* "Whoever loves money never has money enough; whoever loves wealth is never satisfied with his income. This too is meaningless. As goods increase, so do those who consume them. And what benefit are they to the owner except to feast his eyes on them?" (Eccl. 5:10–11).

6. "The No. 1 criteria in every C.E.O. search we do today is integrity," said the senior chairman of a top executive-search company. "That used to be assumed. No one had to mention it. Not anymore." David Leonhardt, "The Imperial Chief Executive Is Suddenly in the Cross Hairs," *New York Times,* June 24, 2002, A17, as business interacted with the collapse of energy, telecommunications, accounting, and retail giants in mid-2002.

7. *Jesus* points out to us in our drivenness and anxiety about growth: "Consider how the lilies grow. They do not labor or spin" (Luke 12:27).

8. In the verse cited above, the lilies do not "spin" their lives thin in busyness.

9. *Paul:* "Command those who are rich in this present world not to be arrogant nor to put their hope in wealth, which is so uncertain, but to put their hope in God, who richly provides us with everything for our enjoyment" (1 Tim. 6:17).

10. *Paul:* "It is required in stewards that one be found faithful" (1 Cor. 4:2 NKJV), not successful or significant by our definition of success or significance.

11. *John:* "Dear friend, I pray that you may enjoy good health and that all may go well with you, even as your soul is getting along well" (3 John 2).

12. *Paul:* You must "be transformed by the renewing of your mind. Then you will be able to test and approve what God's will is—his good, pleasing and perfect will" (Rom. 12:2).

13. *Solomon:* In the journey of life, "Two are better than one, because they have a good return for their work; If one falls down, his friend can help him up. But pity the man who falls and has no one to help him up! . . . a cord of three strands is not quickly broken" (Eccl. 4:9–12)

Chapter 2: Focused Vision

1. From Moses' prayer in Psalm 90:12.

2. *Job:* "Man's days are determined; you [God] have decreed the number of his months and have set limits he cannot exceed" (Job 14:5).

3. *Moses:* Deuteronomy 32:29 is a call to Israel and her enemies, "If only they were wise and would understand this and discern what their end will be!"

4. *Jesus:* Several passages carry the theme of faithfulness and wisdom in life stewardship (e.g., Luke 12:35–48) but all without worrying (Luke 12:22ff).

5. *Paul:* The entire passage of Ephesians 5:1–21 powerfully contrasts the believer from the unbeliever's lifestyle. "Be very careful, then, how you live—not as unwise but as wise, making the most of every opportunity, because the days are evil" (Eph. 5:15–16).

6. *Solomon* makes this clear: "Moreover, when God gives any man wealth and possessions, and enables him to enjoy them, to accept his lot and be happy in his work—this is a gift of God. He seldom reflects on the days of his life, because God keeps him occupied with gladness of heart" (Eccl. 5:19–20). And almost immediately he adds, "God gives a man wealth, possessions and honor, so that he lacks nothing his heart desires, but God does not enable him to enjoy them, and a stranger enjoys them instead. This is meaningless, a grievous evil" (Eccl. 6:2).

7. *Jesus:* "For out of the heart come evil thoughts, murder, adultery, sexual immorality, theft, false testimony, slander" (Matt. 15:19).

8. *Paul* in 1 Timothy 6:19.

9. Leon Morris, *The Gospel According to John, The New International Commentary on the New Testament* (Grand Rapids: Eerdmans, 1971), 719–20.

10. Numerous passages point to the providence of God in personal life as well. Just in the book of Genesis we see God's providence in Noah's salvation (Gen. 7:1), Abraham's call (Gen. 12:1), protection (Gen. 20:3–6, including Sarah and Abimelech), Lot's deliverance (Gen. 19), Isaac's care (Gen. 26:2–3), Joseph's mission (Gen. 39:2–3, 23; 45:7–8; 50:20; cf. Ps. 105:17–22), and Pharoah's warning of famine (Gen. 41). The climax of 50:20, "You meant it to evil, but God meant it to good," undeniably shows God's presence, direction, and control of Joseph's life. You may want to study the instances of God's providence with a good Bible dictionary and commentary—a most amazing testimony to God's goodness in the *personal* lives of His people.

Chapter 3: Soul Vision, Sole Vision

1. J. C. Evans on Percival Lowell, http.physics.gmu.edu/classinfo/astr103/CourseNotes/ECText/Bios/Lowell.htm, Copyright 1995

2. For the intentional journey, vision is more important than willpower. "We do not come to see, however just by looking but by training our vision through the metaphors and symbols that constitute our central convictions." Stanley Hauerwas, *Vision and Virtue* (Notre Dame, Ind: Univ. of Notre Dame Press, 1981), p. 2.

3. Distinguishing *mission* from *vision* reflects my uncomplicated attempt to address the theological discussion on the purpose of God in the Bible as doxological (mission) and soteriological (vision).

4. A summary of a "biblical theology of world missions" follows. I point you to several fine resources for a detailed study of God's vision for the world, especially from the older works by George Peters, *A Biblical Theology of Missions* (Chicago: Moody, 1972) or Roger Hedlund, *The Mission of the Church in the World: A Biblical Theology* (Grand Rapids: Baker, 1991). While the word *mission* is not found in Scripture, the concept of "being sent," from the Latin *missio,* clearly is seen in Scripture. God's vision should also become our mission. We are sent!

5. For Hebrew students: The covenant is found in the *niphal* passive stem and in the *Hithpael* reflexive stem later. The *international* emphasis can be discerned in covenant repetition (Gen. 18:17,18; 22:18; 26:4; 28:14).

6. I could add to this discussion God's working in Melchizedek (Gen. 14:18) and Abimelech (Gen.

20) to prove a non-Abrahamite, international pattern in early human history. The story of Job, most likely placed in the period of the patriarchs, may also show international design. Some scholars see Job's three friends as non-Abrahamite advisers. Further, Joseph's testimony and blessing in Egypt (Gen. 37–50) continues the internationality of the patriarchal period in divine implementation of the covenant.

7. By the way, God causes an exodus parallel of liberating other nations as well—Philistines from Caphtor and Arameans from Kir (Amos 9:7).

8. A theology of the "alien" in the Old Testament confirms their priestly kingdom identity and activity. Israel was not to mistreat (Exod. 22:21) aliens but provide for (Deut. 14:29) and protect (Deut. 24:14–17) them. God even established systemic welfare for the alien (Deut. 14:28–29). The Sabbath was to refresh the foreigner (Exod. 23:12). The foreigner was to keep the Lord's statutes (Lev. 22:18) and would rejoice at the place where God chooses to establish His name (Deut. 16:11). Alien relationships were all part of the *international* witness.

9. We sometimes hear of the total destruction of the Canaanites, but we also must remember that an entire generation of Israelites was wiped out in the wilderness (Deut. 2:15). God's international Vision does not dodge sin committed by Israel or the nations. When you do a theology of the nations in Deuteronomy, Israel and the nations were used by God alternatively to threaten and testify to each other of God.

10. Matthew 28:18–20; Mark 16:15 (if you hold to an authentic longer ending); Luke 24:46–47; John 20:21; Acts 1:8. Jesus confines His disciples to Israel in Matthew 10:5 in order to fulfill His messianic role and program before He prophesies that the kingdom will be taken away from Israel (Matt. 21:43). After the Resurrection, Jesus commissions them to go and make disciples of all nations (Matt. 28:18–20).

11. Klaus Bockmuehl, *Listening to the God Who Speaks: Reflections on God's Guidance from Scripture and the Lives of God's People* (Colorado Springs: Helmers & Howard, 1990), 102. He uses the priorities of the Lord's Prayer—the first three petitions concerned with God's name, kingdom, and will—and only then comes "the material means of subsistence for which we labour in our vocations." To reverse the priorities is to become pagan.

Chapter 4: A Theology of Guidance

1. June Fleming, *Staying Found: The Complete Map and Compass Handbook,* sec. ed. (Seattle: Mountaineers, 1994), 6.

2. Ibid., 6.

3. Sir Martin Rees, Royal Society Professor at Cambridge University, discusses Einstein's thirty-year vain (and premature) quest for a unified theory. "Will such a theory, reconciling gravity with the quantum principle, and transforming our conception of space and time, be achieved in coming decades? And if it is, what answer will it offer to another of Einstein's questions: 'Did God have any choice in the creation of the world?'" From "Minds Meet Online to Offer New Perspectives on Old Questions," *New York Times,* January 9, 2001, D5.

4. We all know and feel the theological tension between the unchangeable purpose of an omniscient God and the reality of human freedom. God's immutable purpose seems to contest human freedom, even though we experientially sense real freedom of choice and take the implications of these choices seriously. To preserve the dimensions of theology and experience, of sovereignty and freedom, my reading of Scripture proposes the following resolution: There is no absolute human autonomy. While we possess the mundane ability to choose freely, we do not possess the moral ability to please God. But in all spheres, mundane and moral, *God knows certainly what we choose freely as we freely choose His certainties.*

5. "For God has put it in their hearts to execute His purpose by having a common purpose, and by giving their kingdom to the beast, until the words of God will be fulfilled" (Rev. 17:17 NASB). Also see Isaiah 19:17; Jeremiah 51:11; Micah 4:12.

6. *Masoretic Text, Psalm 139:14*— "Because I am awesomely distinct/marvelous; your works are extraordinary/marvelous." A complex textual problem with a compound preposition exists here. Internal evidence and the near impossibility of explaining the origin of the MT points me in the way of this meaning.

7. Biological discussion summarized from Sandra Blakeslee, "Some Biologists Ask 'Are Genes Everything?' " *New York Times,* September 3, 1997, B7, B13.

8. *Ibid.* Blakeslee pits holistic biologists against reductionist scientists. If the reductionist view is right, then we can change the genetic composition of an organism to produce whatever we want, fouling up our relationship with each other, "turning everything in life into a commodity. It encourages me to think of you as just a bunch of cells or genes. [Instead, holistic biologists see that] . . . organisms are not merely survival machines. They assume intrinsic value, having worth in and of themselves, like works of art."

9. See the rich use of the "divine book" metaphor in Exodus 32:32–33; Nehemiah 13:14; Psalms 69:28; 87:6; 130:3; and Daniel 7:10.

10. Another "pregnant" theme of God's purposes for "individual futures" beginning from the womb on. See Job 10:8–9; Psalms 22:10; 71:5–6; Isaiah 49:1; and Jeremiah 1:5.

11. A key problem, for without a personal, theistic framework for *personal* purpose, every human being is merely an instrument in relation to others—an issue with "heaven's errand boy" persuasion. Brilliantly illustrated by the Quinten Quist character in Harry Mulisch's mammoth novel (730 pp.), *The Discovery of Heaven,* trans. by Paul Vincent (New York: Viking, 1996).

12. "The LORD Almighty [is] wonderful in counsel and magnificent in wisdom" (Isa. 28:29). God's *counsel* relates to His guidance in the situation; His revelation connects with His purposes from eternity. For example, Jehoshaphat invites Ahab not to be impulsive nor independent but to "please inquire first for the word of the LORD" (1 Kings 22:5 NASB)—ongoing guidance. Yet in Jeremiah 32:19, 23: "Great are your purposes and mighty are your deeds. . . . but . . . they did not do what you commanded them to do"—they did not thwart God's purposes nor receive the benefit of cooperating with them.

13. I link the *everlasting,* eternal way (Ps. 139:24) to its neighboring concept of God's *preordained,* eternal book (v. 16) as the clearest interpretation of the verse. I also translate verse 17 as "how precious to me are your purposes, O God! how vast is the sum of them (i.e., your purposes)!"

14. This list is limited to Jesus' own declaration of His purpose: To fulfill the Law and the Prophets (Matt. 5:17); to glorify the Father (John 17:4); to preach (Mark 1:38); to call sinners (Matt. 9:13) to repentance (Luke 5:32); to preach the Good News to the poor, proclaim freedom, heal the blind, release the oppressed, proclaim Jubilee (Luke 4:18–19); to preach the Good News of the kingdom of God (Luke 4:43); to bring life bread (John 6:51); to dispense abundant life (John 10:10); to judge the world (John 9:39); as a light so "no one who believes in me should stay in darkness" (John 12:46); to save the world (John12:47); to serve and give His life as a ransom for many (Matt. 20:28; cf. Mark 10:45); to suffer (Luke 24:26; John 12:27–28); to bring salvation to Israel (Matt. 15:24); to seek and to save the lost (Luke 19:10); to save the world (John 3:13–17). Some New Testament manuscripts emphasize Jesus' self-consciousness early in life when He chided His parents for worrying about Him, "Did you not know that I must be about My Father's business" (Luke 2:49 NKJV). As mentioned before, His "Father's business" led Him throughout His life: "I have brought you glory on earth by completing the work you gave me to do" (John 17:4).

15. Individual appointments to God's service include Abraham (Gen. 12:1–3; Heb. 11:8–10); Moses (Ex. 3–4), Aaron and his family (Exod. 28:1; Heb. 5:4); Joshua (1:1–9); Gideon (Judg. 6:11–16); Samuel (1 Sam. 3:4–10); Solomon (1 Chron. 28:6–10); Jehu (2 Kings 9:6–7; 2 Chron. 22:7); Cyrus (Isa. 45:1); Amos (7:15); Mary (Luke 1:26–38); the twelve apostles and Paul were chosen and called for special purposes (see Matt. 4:18–22 and parallel passages in Mark and Luke; John 15:16; Acts 9:4–16; 13:2–3; and the first verses of many of Paul's epistles: Rom. 1:1; 1 Cor. 1:1; 2 Cor. 1:1; Gal. 1:1; Eph. 1:1; Col. 1:1; 1 Tim. 1:1; 2 Tim. 1:1). Indeed, we theologically extrapolate from this pattern of individual purpose that though personal purposes differ, God has a special, personal, *ministry* purpose for every believer within His ultimate purpose. (See also note 16 below.)

16. Though classical Greek literature carries different and sometimes contradictory nuances, we are not able to make a hard and fast distinction between God's *will* and *purpose,* for in the New Testament "there is widespread alternation between the two on stylistic grounds." See G. Schrenk, in *Theological Dictionary of the New Testament,* ed. G. Kittel, G. W. Bromiley, and G. Friedrich (Grand Rapids: Eerdmans, 1964), 1:636.

17. Ibid, 633.

18. "The will of God as a superstructure for God's intervention in the affairs of humankind and for all of life was a belief that shaped much of the early church's outlook on theology and life." Philip H. Towner, "Will of God," *Evangelical Dictionary of Biblical Theology*, ed. Walter A. Elwell (Grand Rapids: Baker, 1996), 820.

Chapter 5: Accessing God's Guidance

1. Other Scriptures bear on this matter:

   a) God makes His way straight for us. "Lead me, O LORD, in your righteousness because of my enemies—make straight your way before me" (Ps. 5:8). (cf. Ps. 107:7, God led them in the straight, right way).

   b) God smoothes obstacles, straightens the road, and directs our paths (Prov. 3:6).

   c) God makes our steps firm: "If the LORD delights in a man's way, he makes his steps firm" (Ps. 37:23). God saves us, puts our feet on a rock, and gives us a firm place to stand (Ps. 40:2).

2. Many Bible students point to David as the speaker in "I will instruct you and teach you in the way you should go; I will counsel you and watch over you," though "watching over you" individually would seem to be a more obvious, functional pointer to deity.

3. Hebrews 10 cites the Septuagint version of Psalm 40:6–8 in ascribing it to Christ.

4. Ibid., Klaus Bockmuehl, for example (see note 10 of chap. 3 above).

5. You may remember that we stated that God has a ministry purpose for each Christian and argued this truth not only from God's *actions* but also from His *nature* as caller, appointer, and commissioner of individuals in the Bible. Biography, of course, supplements clear biblical statements for theological conclusion.

6. I take God's anointing in 1 John 2:27 to refer to the Holy Spirit Himself, whose witness attests our sonship (Rom 8:15–16) and enables our convictions and application of truth (cf. 2 Cor. 1:21 22; 1 John 2:20), because those who are led by the Spirit of God are sons of God (Rom. 8:14; Gal. 5:18).

7. Look at what God did for Samuel: "The LORD continued to appear at Shiloh, and there he revealed himself to Samuel through his word" (1 Sam. 3:21). God and His Word will never be at variance.

8. We could develop a biblical theology of "walking in God's ways." Walking in God's ways is a theme I equate to living out God's purpose in an ongoing, vital spiritual relationship with Christ. If Christ is the way and the life (John 14:6), He becomes the way to life and provides the way of life. He is the way of our vital, spiritual walk (Col. 2:6). Religions, especially Buddhism, are quick to point out that they too propose a way of life. Without a way to life, a way of life disorients, confuses, and frustrates the pilgrim.

Chapter 6: Finding God's Will

1. Other direct statements of God's will relate to human salvation (2 Pet. 3:9); giving thanks (1 Thess. 5:18); Spirit-filled controlled vitality (Eph. 5:1–21, esp. v. 17); and a consecrated life (Rom. 12:1–2). Of course, like submissive slaves, we have to do the will of God from the heart (Eph. 6:6).

2. In an excellent book that extols the adequacy of God's Word for living life, the author emphasizes "God's moral will" over the active leadership of the Spirit. "In those areas where the Bible gives no command or principle (nonmoral decisions), the believer is free and responsible to choose his own course of action" (Garry Friesen, *Decision Making and the Will of God*, Portland, Oreg.: Multnomah, 1980) 151. I would add the words "by the leadership of the Spirit." To make it necessary for Christians to "make wise decisions on the basis of spiritual expediency" assumes a great deal of maturity from spiritual morons like myself and seems to suggest that the better you know Scripture, the less you need the Holy Spirit for spiritual direction. They work in tandem. Friesen helps us avoid treating the Bible as a road map. Instead, as indicated in the text it functions like a compass to weather life under the Captain's guidance who can make life straight but not necessarily soft (Prov. 3:5–6). The music group R.E.M. in their song "Stand" sing the words: "If you are confused, check with the sun; Carry a compass to help you along." For Christians, the "sun" is God—always operational, unless we get out from its shining light. The Bible is our Compass—always effective, unless we don't consult it often enough.

3. Quoting Fred Smith, my mentor, the day we celebrated his entry into his eighth decade. He recalled the sentiment of medieval spirituality to that effect. "Who wants a road map, when you have a guide?" he asked. Fortunately, we have both Scripture and God's Spirit for our guidance needs.

4. Acts 13:36 can be understood in three ways: "by the purpose of God he served in his own generation," or "he fulfilled the purpose of God in his own generation," or that "he died (and did see corruption, cf. Messiah) because of the divine counsel." The first and latter options state the obvious. Along with numerous translators, I pick the middle meaning. That also serves my writing purpose that David fulfilled God's purpose in his generation!

5. This confusion of *purpose* and *role* lends to the debate, the charges and countercharges between those who hold to "the way of wisdom" and "God's subjective guidance." The way of wisdom from the Word of God is absolutely clear as to God's purpose. It provides the parameters within which several options may be pursued. On the other hand, as to one's unique role, the leadership of the Lord arises from spiritual discernment of the Word in understanding past, present, and future circumstance. Spiritual sensitivity is the only way to receive wisdom *and* power in taking the way of wisdom, even to make decisions in nonmoral spheres. Write this slogan on your heart: "No obedience, no direction."

6. "Living for the pleasure of God" orientates our lives into a godly focus—again, a dimension of spiritual passion: "We are not trying to please men but God, who tests our hearts" (1 Thess. 2:4); "God is pleased when we do good and share with others" (cf. Heb. 13:16); doing the "things that are pleasing in His sight" (1 John 3:22 NKJV). Enoch is commended as one who pleased God (Heb. 11:5), as is the Lord Jesus, "This is My beloved Son, in whom I am well pleased" (Matt. 3:17 NKJV).

7. I see the yielding, complying, aligning "aspects" of personal will to God's will arising from the volitional aspect of the *thelo* set of Greek words for "will."

Chapter 7: Personal Response—Renovating Life

1. From "Fly Right", *New York Times Magazine* (May 25, 1997): 18.

2. While leadership instructors use "vision" comprehensively to define "a person's chosen course in life" (cf. *Life Vision* [Arlington, Tex.: Creative Leadership Ministries, 1988], 14), I specifically relate personal vision to a person's chosen course of life in accomplishing God's Vision, how we go about His plans for the world.

3. The distinction between the Christian idea of "bearing fruit" and the non-Christian idea of "difference making" lies in the orientation and alignment to the Vision. You can read the latter achievement in year-end issues like "The Lives They Lived," a special issue of the *New York Times Magazine* (December 29, 1996), tracing the lives of forty-seven unusual people who "responded to discovery, distinction, even disgrace" (p. 13). We laud their efforts in making the world a better place. Christians can pursue these achievements under biblical passion, mission, and vision with incredible enthusiasm for *better* betterment of the world.

4. The Greek word order in John 15:5 puts "nothing" at the end of the sentence—its way of screaming capitalization and exclamation for emphasis.

5. "People do not really want to be devoted to Jesus, but only to the cause He started. . . . If I am devoted solely to the cause of humanity, I will soon be exhausted and come to the point where my love will waver and stumble. But if I love Jesus Christ personally and passionately, I can serve humanity, even though people treat me like a 'doormat.'" Oswald Chambers, *My Utmost for His Highest* (Grand Rapids: Discovery House, 1963), June 19. The Suffering Servant of Isaiah bemoans, "I have labored to no purpose; I have spent my strength in vain and for nothing" (Isa. 49:4a). We separate purpose from results, for personally desirable results are not inevitable. We take comfort in the Servant's confidence, "yet what is due me is in the LORD's hand, and my reward is with my God" (v. 4b).

6. Chambers, *My Utmost for His Highest*, April 23.

7. See, for example, the superb work by Michael Novak, *Business As a Calling: Work and the Examined Life* (New York: Free Press, 1997).

8. Especially the predominant view of "calling" among non-Christian spiritual counselors (e.g., Carol

Adrienne, *The Purpose of Your Life;* James Hillman, *The Soul's Code;* James Redfield, *The Celestine Prophecy*) holds that "each person enters the world called." This position is quite different from the biblical view that each person enters the world spiritually dead and must be called into spiritual awakening before receiving direction for life from God, the Awakener, Designer, and Director.

9. "There is not one NT reference in which the language of calling is used of anyone other than the apostles unless the calling is to salvation," summarizes Paul V. Harrison in "Pastoral Turnover and the Call to Preach," *Journal of the Evangelical Theological Society* 44, No. 1 (March 2001): 100. Certainly, an overstatement, Harrison mixes "call" and "calling" to arrive at his conclusion. He concludes, "There is no clear Biblical evidence for what is commonly referred to as a call to preach" (p. 104). Except we will see that preaching (and even plumbing) can be turned into a personal ministry calling under certain conditions and criteria.

10. Paul seems to view marriage as a calling as well in 1 Corinthians 7 but quickly moves into the salvation sense of calling.

11. Chambers, *My Utmost for His Highest,* March 11.

Chapter 8: Reorienting Your Life—Focusing Personal Vision

1. The sturdy chapel at the University of West Indies in Kingston, Jamaica, was once a sugar boiling plant in Trelawny. It too was deconstructed brick by brick, moved, and reconstructed at a new location for a different purpose. Unfortunately, nothing has been done for the All Ethiopian Trade Union building in Addis Ababa, where toilet windows welcome visitors to an otherwise impressive edifice.

2. This sketch was developed in my Spiritual Life classes in conjunction with the Spiritual Formation material proposed by the Center for Christian Leadership at Dallas Theological Seminary. These are not highly dependent on nor derived from the several theories of human development that are presently available (cf. James W. Fowler and Sam Keen, *Life Maps: Conversations on the Journey of Faith,* ed. Jerome W. Berryman [Waco: Word, 1985]). The simplicity of this sketch model allows for personal description, reflection, discovery, and implementation without the accompanying paralysis of analysis that often puts one in the confines of introspection. I do acknowledge the contribution of adult development theorists in the value of crafting and nurturing vision as a critical component of a meaningful adulthood.

3. Interestingly, Hans Markowitsch of the Max Planck Institute for Neurological Research in Cologne, Germany, identifies four distinct memory systems in our brain, each specializing in a different type of information. In this exercise you will be accessing the "episodic" or "autobiographical" memory systems that contain all of our personal experiences. Events strongly bound to our emotions are well anchored here (from Markowitsch, "The Man Who Lost His Self," *World Press Review* [June 1997]: 36).

4. "Oops, we forgot to give Tugger a treat on his birthday" said my daughter sadly. Except, Tugger (our dog) did not know, remember, or experience remorse at that oversight! "Regret," another marker in the lengthy list distinguishing humans from animals, provides a way for humans to discover personal purpose.

5. Chambers, *My Utmost for His Highest,* June 22.

6. "Fighting a Hostile Takeover," a laudable article on Jewish investor Michael Milken who, "having survived prison, the financier is investing in a cure for prostate cancer, before it becomes his death sentence," demonstrates the "scar to mission" process even among non-Christians. By Tom Teicholz, *New York Times Magazine* (June 5, 1994): 34–37.

7. Chambers, *My Utmost for His Highest,* July 6. And I might add that God convinces us of our usefulness by battering us into the shape of the vision *repeatedly!*

Chapter 9: Processing Your Present—Tools for Vision

1. The Wagner-Modified Houts Questionnaire on *Finding Your Spiritual Gifts* (self-published by C. Peter Wagner, 1995) carries a list of twenty-five biblical gifts with fine definitions, some from narratives (e.g., missionary, intercession) outside the four biblical passages, and leaves out others

(e.g., apostleship). Consult a tool like this for self-understanding, knowing that: (1) some gifts cross the "speaking-serving" divide; (2) you may possess gifts on both sides; and (3) new gifts may be given or grown out of your present set of gifts.

2. Ibid., 8.

3. John Piper's book, *Desiring God: Meditations of a Christian Hedonist* (Sisters, Oreg.: Multnomah, 1996), raises many questions. But its central thesis stands as it relates to our ministry satisfaction. While people can justify many penchants, sentiments, and narcissisms, enjoying God's pleasure in His ownership of one's ministry brings us delight as well.

4. One of the most significant insights that my mentor, Fred Smith, shared with me as I struggled with receiving unnecessary and extravagant praise: "They are recognizing the gift. Don't confuse it with your person! And we are not the pump, just the pipe."

5. Again, there are many tools to assess temperament and personality. *Biblical Personal Profiles* by Ken Voges (Minneapolis: Carlson Learning Co., 1992); the *Keirsey Temperament Sorter* based on the book *Please Understand Me* by David Keirsey and Marilyn Bates (Del Mar, Calif.: Prometheus Nemesis Books, 1995); the Birkman Method by Roger W. Birkman are widely used tools for self-understanding and team building. www.2h.com carries hilarious and serious personality tests!

6. Cf. Gail Sheehy, *New Passages: Mapping Your Life Across Time* (New York: Random House, 1995). Also, her *Understanding Men's Passages: Discovering the New Map of Men's Lives* (New York: Random House, 1998).

Chapter 10: Processing Your Present—Opportunity Inventory

1. Cartoon from Taine, Bulls Press, Frankfurt found in the *World Press Review* (January 1995): 23.

2. David Hazard, "His Ways, Our Ways: Trusting God to Shape Our Lives," *Discipleship Journal 95* (1996): 47.

Chapter 11: Processing the Future—Living Your Personal Vision

1. Cf. Stephen Covey, *The Seven Habits of Highly Effective People: Restoring the Character Ethic,* (New York: Simon & Schuster, 1989), First Fireside Ed., 96–97.

2. Quotations from various authors in "Strategy: It's More than a Game," *Life@Work Journal* 1, no. 5 (October 1998).

3. Narrated in "The Perils of Percentages," *The Economist* (April 18, 1998): 70.

Conclusion

1. Morris Dickstein, quoting Kenneth Tynan "An Outsider in His Own Life," review of *Samuel Beckett: The Last Modernist* by Andrew Cronin (New York: HarperCollins, 1997), in the *New York Times Book Review* (August 3, 1997): 11–12.

2. Ibid., 11.

3. Flip Wilson humorously enacts Columbus telling Queen Isabella: "If I don't discover America, there's not gonna be a Benjamin Franklin or a "Star-Spangled Banner," or a land of the free or a home of the brave—and no Ray Charles." When the queen hears this, she screams, "Chris, go and find Ray Charles! You're goin' to America on that boat. What you say!" Mel Watkins obituary to "Flip Wilson, Outrageous Comic and TV Host, Dies at 64," *New York Times* (November 27, 1998, C9).

4. This series applies a theology of spiritual development rather than a psychology of human development, for "not even the best laid developmental scheme can be determinative of human development potential. Christ's grace works in human lives, and that grace is capable of exploding any developmental scheme." William A. Dembski, "Christology and Human Development," *Foundations* (winter, 1997): 14.

5. *Cathy, Dallas Morning News,* July 14, 1994, 9C.

6. Quoted by William D. Boyd, *Houston Bible Institute Newsletter* (December 1993): 1.

7. Henry Wadsworth Longfellow, "Mezzo Cammin," Boppard on the Rhine, August 25, 1842, in *American Poetry: The Nineteenth Century.* John Hollander selected the contents and wrote the notes (New York: Library of America, 1993,) 382.

About the Author

Dr. Ramesh Richard is a professor at Dallas Theological Seminary, where he teaches expository preaching, the spiritual life, and worldview apologetics. He is also the founder and president of *RREACH* International, through which God has permitted him to serve as a global spokesman for the Lord Jesus Christ.

RREACH is an acronym for Ramesh Richard Evangelism and Church Helps. A global proclamation ministry, the vision of *RREACH* is to change the way *one billion individuals* think and hear about the Lord Jesus Christ. Its mission is to "proclaim the Lord Jesus Christ worldwide, with a strategic burden for strengthening the pastoral leaders and evangelizing the opinion leaders of weaker economies."

From his platform at *RREACH*, Dr. Richard travels throughout the world, clarifying the message of the Bible. His audiences are wide-ranging—from non-Christian intellectuals at Harvard University to poor pastors in Haiti, from gatherings of a few to a hundred thousand. In recent years he has been speaking to crowds of men about their spiritual responsibilities in stadiums across the United States. The Lord has given him the opportunity to train thousands of church leaders in more than seventy countries to preach, live, and think biblically. He also has the privilege of exposing society's "opinion leaders" to the Lord Jesus Christ. Each New Year's Day he presents the gospel on prime-time, secular television to large numbers of English-speaking, internet-active audiences in about one hundred countries.

A theologian, philosopher-expositor, evangelist, and author, Dr. Richard holds a Th.D. in Systematic Theology from Dallas Theological Seminary, and a Ph.D. in Philosophy from the University of Delhi.

He lives in the Dallas, Texas, area with his wife, Bonnie, their children, Ryan, Robby, and Sitara.

Order Dr. Ramesh Richard's

"Life Rocks"

DVD/Video summary of

THE INTENTIONAL LIFE

from RREACH International
www.rreach.org

5500 West Plano Parkway, Suite 100, Plano, TX 75093
Telephone: 972-733-3402; Fax 972-733-3495;
E-mail: info@rreach.org

Books #1 & #2 of
The Intentional Life Trilogy

ISBN: 0-8024-6460-2

Soul Passion is a response to the need Dr. Ramesh Richard sees for believers to pursue a purpose so lofty and yet so solid that the shifting sands of daily life will never be able to keep us from living each day in light of our soul passion, our ultimate purpose.

ISBN: 0-8024-6461-0

Soul Mission continues the exciting adventure that began in Soul Passion, Book One of the Intentional Life Trilogy.

Through his wide-angle lens of international travel, his eye firmly on the compass of biblical truth, Dr. Richard leads his readers on a not-to-be-missed literary hike through familiar terrain, making it seem like the first time ever. Get on board!
> Howard G. Hendricks, Distinguished Professor, Chairman, Center for Christian Leadership, Dallas Theological Seminary

MOODY
PUBLISHERS

THE NAME YOU CAN TRUST.

1-800-678-6928 www.MoodyPublishers.org

SOUL VISION TEAM

ACQUIRING EDITOR
Greg Thornton

COPY EDITOR & INTERIOR DESIGN
The Livingstone Corporation

BACK COVER COPY
Paige Drygas, The Livingstone Corporation

COVER DESIGN
UDG| DesignWorks

COVER PHOTO
Getty Images

PRINTING AND BINDING
Quebecor World Book Services

The typeface for the text of this book is
Sabon